KT-483-863

This is the inspiring story of a committed English lady and the orphanage she founded in the ancient city of Solo in Central Java, Indonesia. I have had the good fortune to visit Beth Shan, to hear the laughter and feel the happiness that pervades it. Anne Dakin's remarkable courage over the years has been well rewarded. She now has a large and devoted family of children whom she has rescued, brought up and educated, many of whom are already making their own lives in the wider world. It is a story of love and dedication – and it has its own share of drama too.

Sir Robin Christopher,
British Ambassador to Indonesia,
1997–2000

Anne Dakin is passionate about obeying the Lord. This book captures well the zeal and commitment of a Christian lady, unknown to most, who displays the power and love of Christ in caring for needy children in Indonesia. Read how the Lord has enabled 'Beth Shan' to be 'a place of refuge' against disease and social rejection for over 150 children in this headline-grabbing nation.

Bill McIlroy
Pastor,
Trafalgar Road Baptist Church,
Horsham

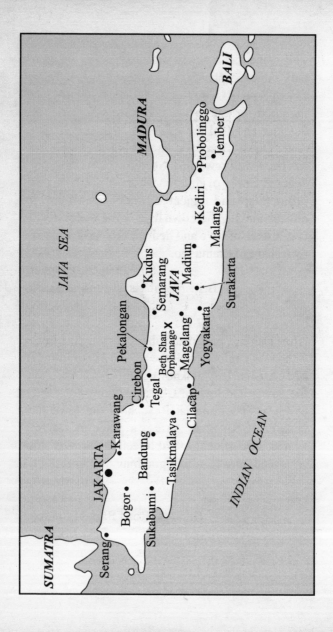

BETH SHAN
A PLACE OF REFUGE

The story of Beth Shan Orphanage in Central
Java where many of Indonesia's children
have found love, security and healing.

KITTY HAY

Christian Focus

To Indonesia's children
and to all who faithfully pray for them
I dedicate this book.

'He who chooses as his permanent abode the
secret place of the most High shall always be
in touch with the almightiness of God' (Psalm
91:1: An Indian dialect version).

All of the author's proceeds from the sale of this
book and donations received will be given to the
work of Beth Shan Orphanage.

© Kitty Hay

ISBN 185792 648 X

Published in 2001 by Christian Focus Publications,
Geanies House, Fearn, Ross-shire, IV20 1TW, Great
Britain.

Cover design by Alister McInnes
Cover photograph by Fin Macrae.
Map © Iain Messider

Contents

ABOUT THE AUTHOR

Kitty Hay was born in Andover in Hampshire in 1932. In her youth she joined a local Methodist Church and in 1948 accepted Jesus Christ as her Lord and Saviour. Following a clear word from God she was baptized by immersion in 1949. Her husband, Allan, died of lung cancer in 1987. After a period of thirteen years within the fellowship of Andover Baptist Church she returned to her Methodist roots in 1998. She has been a local preacher for over forty years and enjoys writing. She has written two brief biographies and for thirteen years wrote a monthly 'Thought for the Month' devotional column for her local newspaper.

At Anne Dakin's invitation she visited Beth Shan for three weeks in July 1990 to research the story of the orphanage. It was a visit that has made a great impact on her life. She is now a member of the Indonesia Prayer Group which meets in Andover every Monday at noon.

ACKNOWLEDGEMENTS

I want to express my thanks to those who helped financially to make my visit to Indonesia possible in 1990. To Sheila Few who first introduced me to Beth Shan and to Elspeth Rodrick for her advice and help. To the Andover Prayer for Indonesia Group who have encouraged me with their love and prayers. To Peter Milsom, Director of The Unevangelised Fields Mission, for wise counsel and prayerful support. To all, some unknown to me, who have faithfully prayed and patiently waited. Above all to Anne Dakin who has entrusted to me the telling of this story of an amazing work of God that has touched and transformed the lives of so many of Indonesia's children.

Some things have had to remain unsaid. Some aspects of the story would have benefited from more research than was possible. My prayer is that in spite of its limitations many who read this book will be prompted to pray and to go on praying.

Preface

I want to express my deepest thanks to all who have worked closely with me at Beth Shan over the years and will ever be a part of the Beth Shan family.

To those who have supported me so faithfully with their prayers and gifts and have helped me to be aware of God when the going has been particularly tough.

To many others whose names do not appear in this book but who have remained alongside me through thick and thin with their loyalty, love and prayers and are all part of the Beth Shan story. You are all very much in my thoughts as I pen these words.

To the intercessors scattered across the globe who continue to uphold me on the frontline.

My special thanks to Audrey Mann and to U.F.M. for their strong support and encouragement and to my mother for her hard work and never wavering support down through the years.

My biggest and very special 'thank you', of course, is to the Lord who took me and began to mould and direct me, bumping me into situations and alongside people who were to have a profound effect upon my life. Take the glory, Lord, for it's all Yours!

And finally to Kitty Hay who has had the responsibility of putting the story of Beth Shan into words.

God bless you all.

Anne Dakin.
Beth Shan Orphanage
1999

Foreword

Anne Dakin is a woman I admire greatly. She is an ordinary person who lives a remarkable life because God has taken hold of her.

Since that never-to-be-forgotten evening when Anne and her Indonesian helper Tutik welcomed Adi, an abandoned baby boy, into their home, hundreds of youngsters have found refuge at Beth Shan. Love and laughter, trepidation, anxiety and relief, anger, resentment and repentance, joy and sadness have all had their place in the tapestry of Anne's life. All of these together with her trust in her utterly dependable and loving heavenly Father are honestly and sensitively narrated.

Anne will want the story of Beth Shan to glorify God, as it does! It is the story of how He sent a young woman to care for Adi and many others like him. To love them, provide them with a home, with food, clothes, education and health care, and above all with the priceless benefit of hearing the good news that the Lord Jesus Christ came into this world to save sinners; that as they trust Him they will have a purpose in life reaching beyond their childhood years, into adulthood and even beyond life itself. As we read these pages we are reminded of our wonderful God, the One Anne loves and serves.

George Rabey
Former General Secretary of U.F.M.
July 2nd, 1999.

1

The Early Years

'If there is anyone here tonight who is willing to go anywhere for God, at any time, will they please stand up.'

Len Moules, on furlough from missionary work on the borders of Tibet, gazed around his young audience, and in the silence that followed his appeal a young girl rose from her seat. As she stood before her friends that night Anne Dakin was totally unaware of the implications of her response, but she knew that God had spoken to her heart.

Anne was the second child of Alan and Dorothy Dakin and was born in Beeston, Nottinghamshire on April 15th, 1942. When she was four years old the family moved to Newquay in Cornwall and it was there that Anne and her two brothers, John and Timothy, spent a very happy childhood.

Her parents were in the hotel business and with their working hours long and busy they decided that they should employ someone to look after the children. In due course Nanny arrived and quickly became part of the family establishing a special place in the lives and affections of all three children.

They attended Sunday School at a nearby Brethren Assembly Hall and Anne's life in particular was influenced by the love and excellent Bible teaching that she found there.

Dorothy Dakin had become a Christian during the first year of her married life and Alan was too much in love with her to stand in her way. They remained deeply in love throughout their married lives and when Anne was eleven years old her father also responded to the claims of Jesus Christ upon his life.

When Anne was in her early teens, with Dorothy's health giving cause for some concern, her father decided that the family should move and they made their new home at The Mill House in Trewerry, about six miles from Newquay. The house was built by John Arundel in 1639, and stood in twenty-two acres of land in the dip of a valley. It was surrounded by Cornish countryside of quite outstanding beauty and Alan hoped that in such a peaceful setting and with a quieter lifestyle Dorothy would soon regain her strength.

The children went to school locally and in her growing-up years Anne's own health problems began to emerge. It was in the classroom, when she was fourteen years old, that she suffered her first 'black-out'. She underwent tests and investigations at Great Ormond Street Hospital but to the great relief of her parents they revealed nothing untoward. It was to prove a weakness that would bother her periodically throughout her adult life and not until much later did she recognise a possible link with times of particular stress.

Every Sunday afternoon Alan Dakin drove the children back to the Assembly Hall in Newquay where they now had many friends, returning to collect them when the evening meeting was over. On Friday evenings he made the trip again so that they could continue to be part of the Young People's Fellowship Group.

Once a month the Y.P.F. travelled almost twenty miles to Redruth Methodist Church to attend a missionary meeting and it was at one of those meetings that Anne responded to God's call upon her life.

She spent most of her teenage years at Trewerry, thrilled with the peace and beauty that was all around her. Her parents were invited to serve as host and hostess to H.M. Judges on the High Court Circuit which entailed a move to Bodmin where they quickly settled and were very happy. By this time Anne had left school and was away from home a great deal, returning for holidays and other occasional visits. Eventually her parents moved to Leicester where they continued with the same kind of work.

In 1961 Anne saw an advertisement for a house-parent in a Christian prayer circular and decided to respond to it. It was the beginning of a relationship with Mrs. Elsie Kohl which was to have a profound influence upon her spiritual life.

Mrs. Kohl and her husband had served as missionaries in China for twenty-seven years until the Communist takeover in 1949 when they were forced to leave the country.

Now widowed, and with her own family grown up, she devoted herself to the care of deprived children in the Brent area of London's East End, working in partnership with Jean André, a Swiss businessman.

Whilst travelling in Europe after World War Two Jean André's heart had been touched by the devastation he saw and by the deep needs of so many traumatized children. By 1961 Jean and his brother had acquired thirty-nine cargo ships, importing and exporting coffee and grain all over the world. They used the profits from their business to buy two houses just a few miles apart in the Jura mountains of Switzerland not far from the French border.

When the houses had been altered and adapted they were able to accommodate a total of 180 children.

Each year Mrs. Kohl arranged for eighty deprived children from the Brent/Kilburn area of London's East End to go to Switzerland in groups of ten, to stay in one of the houses for six weeks. They benefited from the clean fresh air and good wholesome food and at the same time were introduced to the message of God's love for them revealed in Jesus. Most of the children were from broken homes and were recommended by social workers in the borough of Brent. As they went to the camps during term-time government law required the employment of qualified teachers plus one house-parent for every ten children. Mrs. Kohl was due to take a party of ten boys and needed someone to travel with her and to act as a housemother to the children during their stay.

Anne was thrilled when she was accepted for the post which led to her first meeting with Jean André and when Mrs. Kohl returned to England six weeks later Anne remained in Switzerland at his request. By this time Jean André's work amongst deprived and damaged children across Europe was almost legendary and for the next ten years Anne remained involved in that work.

Later, in retrospect, she recognised the importance of those years as God prepared her for a unique and special role among the children of Central Java.

Anne stayed in Switzerland for two years working with Jean Andre before moving on to a hospital in Lausanne to gain some nursing experience. When she eventually returned to England it was to work again alongside Mrs. Kohl, helping her in follow-up work with the children who had been to the Swiss camps. Elsie Kohl was by now very elderly and before long Anne took over from her the reins of the Swiss Outreach work, believing at that time that this was to be her life's work.

She joined a Brethren Assembly in the Portabello Road and taught a class of under-fives in the Sunday School, a work which she thoroughly enjoyed. She shared with them stories about children living in the Philippines who had never heard of Jesus, and together they discussed ways to help these children who did not have Bibles from which they could learn.

Some of the children wanted to send 'Jesus books' to them, but Anne explained that they spoke a different language and would not be able to understand stories written in English.

The weeks passed and the children still clamoured for more stories about the children of the Philippines until Anne knew the favourite ones almost by heart!

One little girl asked if they could send their pennies, and a collecting box was quickly found. Copper coins, and often silver too, were brought along each week, with mounting excitement as they tested how heavy the collecting box was becoming.

In a World Outreach magazine Anne found the address of a New Zealand girl named Carol Walker who was working as a missionary in the Philippines. With the eager consent of the children she forwarded to her the money they had collected and asked in return for photographs of children for whom they could pray.

As she continued to send money to Carol Walker she mentioned in a letter that she was seeking God's guidance for her own future and asked for her prayers. She also spoke about it to Mrs. Kohl, knowing that she could rely on her sound counsel and faithful prayer support.

Anne's work with the Jean André Homes and her links with World Outreach continued until 1970 when it became clear that God was drawing that particular chapter in her life to a close.

In April 1970, returning with a group of children from her final trip to Switzerland she found a letter waiting for her and felt strangely excited as she opened it.

It was from Carol Walker who was writing to tell her that her parents, Dal and Dorothy Walker, were serving as missionaries in Indonesia and were looking for someone to teach their eight-year-old son, Brent, with the help of a New Zealand correspondence course. From Carol they had learnt a great deal about Anne and were convinced that she was God's choice. Would she prayerfully consider the matter?

As she prayed Anne recognised God's hand and wrote back eagerly accepting their invitation.

2

INDONESIA

Background information

Indonesia is the world's largest archipelago and has a beauty all its own. It is made up of some 13,670 islands along the equator with approximately 6,000 of them inhabited. From east to west it stretches across 3,200 miles of ocean and from north to south covers an area of 1,200 miles. This vast span of islands boasts a total of 330 ethnic groups and 250 distinct languages.

Of its many islands the five main ones are Sumatra, Kalimantan, Sulawesi, Irian Jaya and Java and it is the fourth most populous country in the world. Java, though not the largest island, is the most densely populated, with more than 60% of the country's population crammed into it.

Indonesia was under Dutch rule from the middle of the 18th century, finally gaining its independence in 1945.

The new Republic of Indonesia elected Sukarno as President in 1945 and following a coup he was replaced by Suharto in 1968.

When Suharto was forced to resign in 1998 Habibie was appointed in his place until Wahid was voted in as President in 1999. Megawati, daughter of Sukarno and very popular with the people was elected vice-president.

Since independence great emphasis has been placed on education and it is now law that all children attend primary school for six years, with many going on to junior and secondary schools and university. Approximately 84% of children of 15 years and over are now literate. All education costs and medical treatment costs have to be paid for by even the poorest families.

Indonesia is now ranked among the world's leading oil exporters and remains, with Brazil, the world's largest producer of tin.

It is fast becoming industrialised with a new focus on raw materials and with oil and natural gas the main sources of export income. Agricultural exports still include spices together with coffee, rubber, tea and quinine. Poor diet, overcrowded housing, lack of sanitation and impure water have all contributed to the country's serious health problems.

The climate is tropical with two monsoon seasons, the wet season from November to March and the dry season from June to

October. Humidity is generally high with a daily temperature range of 20 to 32 degrees centigrade.

Indonesia has more than 200 active volcanoes resulting in rich volcanic soil which is ideal for growing crops.

In spite of intensive logging in recent years about two thirds of the land area remains covered by forest. Valuable woods produced include ebony, teak and bamboo. Next to oil and gas, timber is now the country's largest single export.

Rice, grown mainly in Java, is still the country's main staple diet, but a large amount still has to be imported to feed such a vast population.

Indonesia's two largest cities are both on the island of Java. Jakarta is the chief centre of commerce and the capital city and Surabaya is next in size and is a busy port. Jakarta has a population of 9 million and a further 2.7 million live in Surabaya.

Although freedom of religion is guaranteed under the Constitution, new laws and amendments continue to give rise to deep concern within the Christian community. Indonesia is the world's most populous Muslim nation and in various forms it is the faith of 87% of the people. 9% are Christian and form the largest of the minority religions. In northern Sulawesi almost 80% of the population are Christians. About 10% of the population practise Buddhism while Hinduism, once the most predominant religion, is now practised by just 2%. Hindu influences, however, remain strong within Indonesian culture. In the more remote areas indigenous religions are still practised.

Indonesia was greatly affected by the Asian financial crisis of the 1990s and international investment was withdrawn in 1997. The financial situation remains on a knife edge and the recent riots and violent demonstrations have radically affected the tourist trade which had become a lucrative source of income.

By January 1998 the value of the rupiah, which is the monetary unit of the country, had dropped dramatically and the financial sector almost collapsed. This economic crisis, especially the withdrawal of subsidies on food prices was the catalyst for the riots and widespread violent demonstrations in May 1998. This also led to the long overdue political changes which rocked the country.

Foreign debt repayments currently claim one third of export profits and are a heavy drain on the nation's budget. Economic development is centred on main islands around Java while smaller islands are impoverished.

Central Java, where the Beth Shan Orphanage is situated, is very beautiful and is home to a variety of exotic plant life and wildlife. Bougainvillaeas are breathtaking in their beauty and grow prolifically, as do many other flowers and shrubs. Species of moths and butterflies, many of them very large, are also a spectacular sight. Paddy fields, rivers, volcanic peaks and rolling hills are all part of the landscape, while in the cities large buildings, ancient monuments, much traffic and bustling activity produce a marked contrast. Some families are affluent but a far greater number live well below the poverty line. Rich or poor they are all proud of their Indonesian identity.

Following the riots and rampages of the late 90s the tension has been almost tangible and in the present uneasy peace fear and apprehension are not far below the surface. The situation at the dawn of a new millennium remains volatile.

3

1972 – 1975

Touchdown

The Yayasan. A visa withheld.
Beth Shan at Baron

Welcome to Indonesia!
How thrilling Dorothy Walker's words
sounded to Anne Dakin's ears as she passed
through the terminal at Yogyakarta Airport.

Although the two women were meeting for
the first time the correspondence of recent
weeks had already forged a bond between
them. Dal and Dorothy Walker were a
missionary couple from New Zealand who had
recently established a Bible School in the
mountain regions of Central Java and Anne had
been accepted for the post of home tutor to their
eight-year-old son, Brent. She had looked
forward eagerly to this first step into her new
life in Indonesia.

Soon, with her luggage loaded into the
waiting jeep, they were on the road, and as the

27

vehicle climbed higher Anne was relieved to feel the air getting cooler. Eagerly she caught her first glimpse of paddy fields and sugar cane plantations, and of small villages scattered on the mountain side. Here and there clumps of trees provided shelter and shade from the intense equatorial heat. Varieties of brightly coloured butterflies captivated her attention as they flitted past and later she would be spellbound by the giant Elephant moth with transparent windows in its wings and a wing span of at least nine inches.

A great wave of excitement swept over her when at last Tawangmangu came into view, nestling half-hidden 3,500 feet up on the slopes of Mount Lawu. She offered a silent prayer of thanksgiving to God. How wonderfully He watched over her throughout the long 7,500 mile journey. Already the memories and mixed emotions of family farewells at Gatwick Airport were less painful and her tiredness vanished as the Javanese believers ran out to welcome her. It was February 17th, 1972.

It would take time to adjust to such a vast change in culture and climate, and for the first few days Anne just lazed around, occasionally sitting in on Brent's lessons. He was a friendly little boy and she was encouraged by his obvious learning ability.

It was the rainy season and Anne had never seen such rain! It was as if the heavens had literally opened! She revelled in the beauty of huge poinsettias, vivid orange trumpet creepers, and the breathtaking colours of the bougain-villaeas. Her love of rice dishes helped her to adjust to a new and strange diet, and growing all around her was an abundance of fresh fruit.

Despite the language barrier and the strangeness of it all she knew in her heart that this was where God wanted her to be. Working with children was clearly going to be a possibility but in order to communicate she must first learn the language.

There was to be no language teacher; working and sharing with the Indonesian people was vital to pronunciation, and grammar would be learnt by comparing Indonesian Bible passages with English.

Gradually she began to settle into the routine of her new life. When temperatures were at their highest she welcomed with relief the 'istirahat siang' (siesta time), and as the weeks slipped by the rain gave way to the dry season, bringing with it parched grass and mud tracks that were dusty and hard as concrete. Language study was not easy in the intense heat but the knowledge that communication was essential spurred her on.

The Javanese people stared at her in amazement. She was tall – very tall by their standards, and her skin was white. They whispered to one another 'Dia tinggi. Dia tinggi' ('She tall. She tall'), pointing with their fingers and giggling loudly.

The Walkers rented a hall further along the road from the Bible School, which was used as a meeting place for the students and when Anne shared with them in Sunday morning worship variations of height and skin colour ceased to matter.

As the service proceeded she became aware of small brown faces peering in through the open doors and windows. With their jet black hair greased with coconut oil these children delighted her. Little girls no more than seven or eight years old struggled along with batik slings in which they carried toddlers too young to walk. Among the superstitious fears that abounded was the belief that evil spirits could attack them if they put their feet on the ground while they were still very young.

Three white grown-ups with sparkling white teeth leading the worship? The children stared in disbelief. Most of the grown-ups they knew could not boast more than six teeth apiece by the time they were thirty, and the few they had were certainly not sparkling white! Chewing the beetle-nut led to unpleasant brown staining and premature decay and the few who could afford to visit the local dentist looked upon him as a man to be feared. His primitive dentistry tended to be very painful!

How tall the white lady in the middle was! How could anyone grow as tall as that? Discussing the matter amongst themselves none too quietly the children started to giggle.

Anne walked slowly back to the Bible School when the service was over. 'One day, Lord', she whispered in her heart, 'With Your help I will care for children such as these.'

She waited impatiently for the arrival of her trunk and the dental equipment she had requested from England. She knew that untold agony could vanish with the removal of a rotten tooth, but for most of the village people of Central Java poverty and fear put the possibility of relief far beyond their reach. Although Anne had learnt basic dentistry at home she had not had the opportunity to practise her skills, and now the opportunities were all around her. But first she would need a work permit.

Not least among her frustrations was the constant battle against mosquitos, a battle she was not likely to win until her body had built up some immunity against them.

In between lessons with Brent and her own language studies the possibility of an orphanage dominated her thinking more and more. She shared her vision with Pontas and Mavis Pardede who were working in the Tawangmangu Bible School, and learnt that they were planning to build a Bible School at Surakarta (Solo) where they hoped eventually to live.

After much prayer they agreed to become Anne's sponsors and over the years that followed their advice and guidance were to prove invaluable. Together they discussed the aims and objectives of the orphanage and the sort of children they would expect to care for. Pontas was a gifted man, highly qualified in the legal profession and a minister of theology. He was Indonesian by birth and well respected in both legal and church circles. The prime concern of both Pontas and Mavis was the spreading of the gospel of Jesus Christ among the Indonesian people.

With the powers of non-nationals in the country very limited Pontas suggested the formation of a Yayasan (Foundation Trust) to oversee all the legal affairs of the proposed orphanage, and to this Anne readily agreed. It was a tentative step forward and she was thrilled. With the possible move of the Pardedes at some future date it seemed wise to consider an orphanage near to the town of Solo. This would provide reasonable access to shops and schools and would also present no major geographical problems to any of her friends and family who might want to visit.

The enormous step she was contemplating would require prayerful and careful consideration, and would signal the end of her close involvement with the Walker family and with Brent's education. The way forward was certain to be challenged and tested and she must be careful to bring to the Lord each new thought and idea that came to her as the vision became clearer. How hard it was to be patient!

'My thoughts are not your thoughts, neither are your ways My ways' (Isa. 55:8). God's words spoken through the prophet Isaiah were to hit her very forcibly before the year ended.

In the meantime Anne was experiencing her first Indonesian Christmas with very mixed feelings. Essentially a family time, her thoughts were frequently with her own family so far away. How good it would be to see them all. This Christmas, so vastly different from celebrations she had previously enjoyed, brought home to her the spiritual needs of

Indonesia's people who for the most part had no idea of the festival's true meaning.

The children of Indonesia were never far from her thoughts; so many of them homeless and unwanted. Pontas and Mavis had recently adopted one such child and had named her Jenny. Her background was tragic and her physical condition poor, but with love and proper care she was already showing signs of improvement. How Anne longed to see other children given the same opportunity to respond to the love and security of a Christian home.

December was almost over when Anne received a letter from the Immigration Office in Semarang, informing her that her visa would not be renewed and she must leave the country by February 2nd, 1973. In spite of urgent prayer requests despatched to England and elsewhere Anne had no choice and at the end of January she flew back to England.

She left most of her possessions stored away at Tawangmangu against the day of her return. She had no idea when that day would be but she knew beyond all doubt that she would be back. She was aware of her need to talk with Dal and Dorothy Walker before she left for she was equally certain that when she did return it would not be to continue as tutor to Brent. How thankful she was that there had been no binding contract of employment.

The knowledge that the Yayasan had now been set up afforded her some comfort and she was happy to rely on Pontas. He would be able to appoint men known to him as Christian leaders, respected in their communities, with various skills to offer that would be of benefit when an orphanage was established. She knew that they, too, would be praying for her return.

Almost two years had passed when Anne once again bade an emotional farewell to her family and friends at Gatwick Airport.

The long months of waiting and uncertainty had not been easy but she knew, too, that they had not been wasted.

There had been those few precious days with Mrs. Elsie Kohl, and Retreats and Conferences where God spoke clearly to her heart. A crash course in tropical medicines had given her further valuable experience in that field as she sought to prepare herself in every way for her return to Indonesia. At last the long-awaited letter from the Embassy arrived – her visa had been granted! It had been a long wait! But now she was airborne and her spirits soared with the plane as it nosed its way higher and higher above the clouds. At last she was on her way back to Indonesia's children with the much prayed for visa safely in her handbag! It was March 15th, 1975.

Arrangements had been made for Anne to live initially with Pontas and Mavis and under their guidance she would explore all possible areas of outreach. As the plane silently swallowed up the miles she contemplated again the practical and legal details that would be involved in establishing an orphanage, and at times the enormity of the project frightened her. She encouraged herself by recalling the very positive response of family and friends in England when she shared her vision with them. She did not visualise a large institutional work but rather a small beginning with a willingness to expand should God so lead.

During the long months of waiting for her visa to be granted Anne had frequently struggled with her Christian faith, and drugs prescribed by her doctor to control occasional 'blackouts' may have been responsible for the bouts of depression that often troubled her.

With constant inner conflict she had felt very miserable in her Christian life, but like a gold thread running right through the middle of all her turmoil the orphanage vision had remained.

She pondered her developing relationship with Pontas and Mavis and the high esteem in which Pontas was held both as a scholar and as an Indonesian citizen.

She thought about the recently formed Yayasan and its ability to act in areas that would be denied to her, particularly in the purchasing of land with all the legal details that involved.

She allowed her thoughts to wander over a possible location, the type of building that would be most suitable and the name she would choose for her home. With these more positive thoughts and reflections she obediently fastened her seat belt as the plane prepared to land at Jakarta Airport.

The intense heat seemed to rise up from the ground to meet her as she made her way towards Customs, but how good it was to be back on Indonesian soil! It was too late to get a flight to Solo so she found herself an hotel room for the night. Her window looked out on a railway track with a scattering of tumbledown shacks and makeshift dwellings on either side, where many of Jakarta's poor and homeless obviously lived.

Everywhere she looked she saw children, ragged and unkempt, playing in the debris which was scattered all around. As she surveyed the scene her heart ached and within her the vision stirred again.

How many of these children would reach

adult life? According to recent statistics it would be less than 50%, as malnutrition, tummy bugs and tuberculosis took their toll. What chance did any child have amid so much filth and squalor? She lay on her bed, concentrating on her vision, and fell asleep.

Pontas and Mavis Pardede were waiting to welcome her at the airport the following day and drove her to their home in the centre of Solo. It was reached by a stony mud road with open sewers on either side where children played barefoot.

Pontas and Mavis now had two small children and Anne knew that she would quickly feel at home with them. It was great to be back and even the mosquitos could not dampen her enthusiasm.

Later, as together they discussed Anne's next step, Pontas suggested that she should look for a house to rent, and begin her work from there until she was in a position to build. They would need to prayerfully consider the location because land prices in some areas had rocketed during her two years in the U.K. In the meantime she would continue to live with Pontas and Mavis. Another Bible School was now being built in Solo and once it was completed they would be moving there to live. Anne planned to devote most of her first year to language study, and accepted an invitation to teach Health and Hygiene to the Bible students, as this would also help to improve her grasp of the language.

Pontas suggested one day that the three of them should begin to look for a suitable property for Anne to rent, rather than Anne having to move with them to the Bible School complex.

Anne's initial reaction was one of total panic. 'Am I doing the right thing?' 'I've no staff and no children.' 'It would be madness to live alone.' That night she slept little.

As she lay in the darkness she concentrated her thoughts on Psalm 91:1 – 'He who dwells in the secret place of the Most High shall abide under the shadow of the Almighty.' She pondered the translation of an Indian dialect version of the same verse which reads 'He who chooses as his permanent abode the secret place of the most High shall always be in touch with the almightiness of God.'

To Anne the words came as a further confirmation of God's continued leading. In the Indonesian language the word 'shadow' is translated 'a place of refuge and safety', and she prayed that the orphanage of her vision might be just that.

She pledged herself to pray for physical,

emotional and spiritual healing for every child God chose to bring to her. She would offer a home, food and education, but above all the opportunity to learn about Jesus Christ and to find a place of refuge close to the heart of God.

A contact of Pontas told him of a two-bedroomed property in the village of Baron which was available to rent and might be suitable. It was a plain white building, typically Javanese in structure, with no running water and no electricity. The floors were tiled, making them cool and easy to clean.

A well outside the back door was about 12 metres deep and offered a supply of very murky water! Due to the dreadful sedimentation it would need to be boiled and then left to settle before it could be used with a reasonable degree of safety.

A man who lived in a shack on the land had planted a garden of peanuts and cassava. He went out each day with his cooking pots swinging from a bamboo cane across his shoulders to sell meatball soup at the roadside.

Pontas, Mavis and Anne were all sure that this house was God's provision and the contract was signed. They were required to pay three years rent in advance, a total of 450,000 rupiahs. According to the rate of exchange in 1975 that was the equivalent of £150 in English money! Anne's emotions were a mixture of excitement and apprehension.

Anne moved in on June 28th, 1975, with one truckload of goods representing her total possessions, and named her home 'Beth Shan'. Her anticipated year of language study would have to wait!

'Tante, where is your husband?' 'How many children do you have?' 'Tante, why are you alone? At night evil spirits will come out; it is not safe to be alone.' Anne was learning to accept the village folk gathered around her open door and peering through her windows. They would squat down wherever there was a space watching wide-eyed as she cooked, did her washing, or drew water from the well.

The arrival of a tall white woman in their midst had been the main topic of conversation for some time and the questions were endless! Unmarried? No children? Alone at night? Such things were unheard of. Some of the time they ignored her, squatting in groups around her door and discussing this strange situation in loud whispers and with much giggling.

In her faltering Indonesian she spoke to them about the God who was always with her and who gave His Son to die for her. 'He died for each one of you, too', she told them, 'so that you could have your sins forgiven and become His children.' They shook their heads as they listened. 'Yes', they repeated to one another, 'she is very strange.'

4

Tutik. Beth Shan's first children.

June – December 1975.

In July Anne accepted an invitation to visit missionary friends in Surabaya in East Java and it was to prove an important visit. She attended a prayer meeting and agreed with some reluctance to share her plans to establish an orphanage. With so many things as yet unclear in her own mind she realised that the questions they would ask might be difficult to answer.

Where is the money coming from? Who will be working with you? When? What? How? The fourteen WEC missionaries listened with great interest as she spoke of the vision God had given her and of His leading thus far, but to all their questions Anne could only reply 'I don't know.'

One of them, Myrtle Whitehead, came across to introduce herself when the meeting was over. She told Anne of a young girl in the town who was a recent convert from Islam and might be a suitable helper for her in the work she was proposing to do. She was facing strong opposition from her family and was prayerfully considering her future. Her Bible had been confiscated and her freedom to attend meetings was greatly restricted. Myrtle suggested that Anne might like to go with her the following day to meet the girl. Her name was Tutik and she was nineteen years old.

The next morning the two women set out by becak (pedicab) to visit Tutik's home, reaching the house just as a young girl and an elderly woman came through the garden gate. Tutik and her grandmother were on their way to market.

Myrtle introduced Anne who briefly outlined her story and her need of a helper. She suggested to Tutik that she should pray about this for a month, and then let her know whether or not she felt God was calling her to get involved.

When Anne returned to her little house in Baron she was confident that whatever the outcome of her conversation with Tutik God had everything under control.

Local news travels fast and the bush telegraph had been busy. Soon the tall white woman would not be alone. Soon there would be lots of children coming to live in her little white house. Eagerly they watched and awaited developments.

Pontas arranged for a circular to be printed giving details of the proposed orphanage, sending out copies with the Bible School's bi-monthly magazine as well as to many of the churches in Central Java. God was on the move!

August was almost over when Anne answered a knock at her door one morning. Standing there, clutching a bag, stood Tutik. 'God told me to come', she said simply, 'so I came.'

From the start Anne and Tutik worked well together and gradually the barriers of culture were broken down. Anne learnt a great deal from the girl as she talked about her family and the varied experiences of her young life, and she was encouraged to see how quickly Tutik adjusted and settled in. Together they began to pray about the future.

They worked hard, cleaning and painting Beth Shan in readiness for the arrival of their first child. Anne firmly believed that every child who came would be brought to them by God, by whatever means He chose to use, confirming that this work was indeed of Him and not something that Anne had brought about.

'I believe that God wants me to go to Madiun today,' Tutik announced quietly at breakfast one morning, taking Anne completely by surprise.

She tried to persuade her to wait a while but her mind was made up. 'I believe God wants me to go today,' she said earnestly, 'so that I can share with my friends what He is doing in my life.'

As soon as they had completed their meal and shared in a time of prayer together Tutik set off, and Anne spent an anxious and uneasy day, finding it impossible to settle to her normal household tasks. Her thoughts were constantly with Tutik, and as darkness fell and the evening wore on her concern increased. Travelling alone by bus could be very dangerous, especially for a young girl.

It was almost nine o'clock when she heard the click of the garden gate and the sound of footsteps coming up the path to her door.

She hurried out and could not disguise her relief when she saw Tutik standing there, a broad smile lighting up her face. She offered Anne the bundle she was carrying in her arms. 'I've brought you your first baby', she announced triumphantly. Gazing up at Anne was a tiny baby boy.

She looked from the baby to Tutik, not certain whether to laugh or cry. A vision is one thing – but when the vision becomes a reality

– well, that's a different matter altogether!

Still clutching the precious bundle she followed Tutik back into the house. A verse of Scripture was buzzing around in her head, 'Take the young child and nurse him for Me' (Exodus 2:9). 'Yes, Lord,' she responded in her heart, 'I most gladly will'.

Later, when their new charge was fed, cuddled and fast asleep, Tutik shared with Anne the remarkable events of her day.

She had arrived in Madiun and was on her way to visit a friend when the inner voice of God spoke clearly to her. 'Turn back. Go and see Dr. Prabowo'. Almost mechanically Tutik had retraced her steps and walked towards the doctor's house. She had previously worked part-time as an assistant midwife and knew him well. Obviously surprised to see her the doctor invited her into his home.

In a few simple sentences Tutik told him her story; how she had become a Christian and how Anne had invited her to become her helper at Baron. She told him about Anne's vision of an orphanage and gave him one of the circulars she had taken with her.

The doctor was listening intently with a look of incredulity on his face. 'This is remarkable', he muttered, more to himself than to Tutik. 'This morning', he told her, 'a baby boy was

47

left on my doorstep. With him was a note asking me to care for him. He is just six weeks old'.

Later, when Tutik left the doctor's home, she was clutching the tiny baby in her arms. How thankful she was that she had obeyed that inner Voice.

The baby's name was Adityokrisnuyudha – so they called him Adi for short!

The drive to Sumarwono across the mountain roads had been a hair-raising experience. The bus was ancient and the driver none too careful, but they had made it! Now a short walk across a field would bring them to their destination. Bambang, Anne's companion, was her pastor and had been appointed as Secretary of the Yayasan. It was as a result of information passed on to him that they had come all this way.

Together they approached a typically Javanese house, with plaited bamboo walls and a curved roof and as Anne stooped to get through the rickety bamboo door the stench of dampness and body odour made her catch her breath. Bambang walked in behind her surveying the scene as his eyes became accustomed to the semi-darkness. Believing the place to be empty they prepared to wait for the return of the child and his kakek (grandfather) when a whimper from the far corner of the room startled them.

Very cautiously they went nearer and discovered a little boy sitting cross-legged on a dirty platform which appeared to serve as his bed. His only bedding was the rotting woven mat on which he sat and flies fed on the squalor all around. His clothes were filthy and he had long outgrown them. A banana leaf was by his side holding a meagre portion of rice and a tin mug half-filled with tea. No doubt he was forced to share his sparse meal with the rats and chicken which were his only companions.

Coming closer, they were able to study the child more carefully. His scalp was black and his hair full of lice. He could not have been washed for a very long time. His head was much too large for his emaciated body and he looked barely human. His stomach was huge, his tiny legs like matchsticks, and his body was covered with sores.

Anne shuddered as she forced herself to look at him and a battle began to rage within her. This was not the sort of child she had pictured so often in her mind and she did not want to be responsible for such a monstrosity. Surely God would not ask so much of her.

An old man, clearly the child's grandfather,

hobbled in through the door. Bambang had been told that he was the only living relative and was forced to sell water from early morning to mid-afternoon to scrape together sufficient money for the two of them to survive. He picked up the boy and carried him through to a little kitchen, but this seemed to distress rather than comfort the child.

The old man told them that the child's name was Suriadi and that his parents had been killed in a local earthquake. Pastor Bambang talked with him about the plight of his grandchild and showed him the papers he would be required to sign if he agreed to place Suriadi in the care of Beth Shan.

Eventually he signed, and gathering up the pathetic child in his arms Bambang left quickly with Anne following close behind.

They went straight to the home of a local pastor where they were given tea and Suriadi was put gently into a bath of water in an attempt to remove some of the grime. It would take a long time to deal with all the ingrained dirt. He sat in a tin tub, dazed and bewildered, while the adults shared a welcome meal of rice and vegetables. When the meal was over Bambang gently dried his swollen body and started to dress him. Several local Christians had arrived to bring what practical help they could and

Anne and Bambang thanked them all before setting off to climb back down the mountain path to the local transport stop.

They clambered aboard the 'transport' which turned out to be a dilapidated old van. Drivers in Indonesia are notoriously reckless, blaming any accident that might occur on 'the will of Allah', and as they careered back down the narrow mountain roads they could only cling to the sides and hold their breath! With great relief they reached Salatiga where they boarded the local bus that would take them home.

The bus was crowded, with baskets of wares stacked in every available spot and live chickens tied by the feet dangling from the roof and protesting loudly at the indignity of it all.

Anne was painfully aware that everyone on the bus was staring at them, first at Bambang, just five feet tall, then at her, at least twelve inches taller. 'He short and black'. 'She tall and white'. 'What a strange child'. The passengers stared and whispered loudly amongst themselves.

It was a ludicrous situation and she could not fail to be amused, but she heaved a sigh of relief when they finally arrived at their stop. With Bambang carrying the little boy they climbed out of the bus and walked the final short distance back to Beth Shan. They were tired and dirty and very glad of a cold drink to quench their thirst. What a day it had been!

Anne looked again at Suriadi. He would not be an easy child to love and care for but God had entrusted him to her and she would do her best.

Bewilderment and confusion threatened to overwhelm the little boy during his early days at Beth Shan. Previously he had spent most of the day alone in semi-darkness and now he was surrounded by people. Gently Anne and Tutik sought to convey to him their love and concern, but he had no idea how to respond. With his body so swollen and sore he could not bear to be touched and anyone coming too close filled him with terror.

Everything was new and different and he could not understand what was happening, so he settled for the only weapon at his disposal, emitting loud piercing shrieks whenever he was approached.

Anne decided that right away he must be treated for worms, and the following morning his nappy was full of a seething mass of roundworms. He whimpered alarmingly and Tutik fled from the house in horror. It would be a long time before the nourishment lost to those foreign bodies could be replaced.

At night he would let out terrifying, blood-curdling yells as if experiencing dreadful nightmares, and as the weeks passed slowly by the nightly disturbances did not lessen. Anne and Tutik became aware that this was a battle with the powers of darkness and was a battle they had to win.

It had been a hot and tiring day when Anne rolled into bed and within minutes she was fast asleep. In the early hours of the morning the house was once again filled with penetrating shrieks, and as she groped her way, half-asleep, to Suriadi's cot the truth of the situation dawned on her. This was a problem that no amount of loving and comforting was going to solve. Taking the child in her arms she rebuked in the Name of Jesus the evil spirits that were tormenting him. The grip of Satan was now apparent and she felt helpless in an unfamiliar situation. Into her mind came the words of Scripture, 'The Name of the Lord is a strong tower; the righteous run to it and they are safe' (Prov. 18:10).

Standing in the middle of the room and speaking with the authority of the Holy Spirit she commanded Satan in Jesus' name to leave the child. She laid Suriadi back in his cot and returned to her bed. The child slept and the nightly episodes did not occur again.

It was late afternoon and the beginning of the rainy season. Suriadi had been at Beth Shan for two weeks and the family had just finished their evening meal when they were startled by a loud knock at the door. Standing on the step was Aniek, Tutik's friend from Madiun, and beside her a young woman holding a sickly looking baby girl in her arms.

The woman poured out her sad story. She had no husband, and with a baby to care for she was not able to work. At fourteen months the little girl was still being fed at the breast but now the supply of milk was inadequate and she was afraid that the child would die. Her name was Munarsih. Would Anne be willing to take her in and care for her?

Anne looked at the pathetic young woman so clearly distressed, and her heart ached for her. The baby's flesh hung in folds on her tiny, wasted body and her weight could not have been above five kilos. Adi, just three months old, weighed more than that.

She invited the little group into Beth Shan and through the night the woman nursed her child on the floor. Early the next morning she left, never to return. Later Anne learnt that she had turned to prostitution in a desperate bid to survive.

Munarsih was suffering from malnutrition

and tuberculosis and for the first three weeks she seldom stopped crying. Gradually, in very small doses, she began to take nourishment and Anne and Tutik noticed with relief that she was beginning to settle down. They were both exhausted.

November 13th dawned amid a flurry of excitement. All the morning people came and went, delivering, organising and checking final arrangements. It was the day of the official opening of Beth Shan.

At four o'clock the visitors began to arrive, coming from various churches and organisations and all with a practical interest and concern for the work. Seventy-five people attended the celebration and the three children behaved perfectly. Protected and held by those they were learning to love and trust they were not overwhelmed by the sudden influx of people.

As Anne gazed around at the visitors, many of whom were now her friends, joy and praise to God welled up in her heart. It was a memorable occasion.

A few days later the scene at Beth Shan was vastly different. There was no cash left and very little food in the cupboard and as Anne pondered how to produce an adequate meal on such slender resources she heard the familiar rattle of the garden gate.

Looking through the window she saw one of the Ibus from the local church walking up the path. She recognised her at once and wondered what had brought her to Beth Shan. The woman had suffered from leprosy for more than twenty years, and was miraculously healed as she listened to Pontas preaching in Solo. It was an open-air meeting and she had decided to go along and as she listened to the message of the gospel God touched her life and she was healed.

She became a Christian, and although the ravages of the disease remained, her face grew radiant and beautiful. She told Anne that she had called to bring a dish of gudeg as a gift for the Beth Shan family. Gudeg consists of chopped young jackfruit cooked in coconut milk and was a dish that Anne did not enjoy. She thought to herself how strange it was that God should provide this food just at the right moment but with a dish that she disliked so much. The thought of the stumps of fingers that had prepared it, however lovingly, seemed to make matters worse. Anne thanked the Ibu graciously and took the gudeg to the kitchen to reheat.

At lunchtime, with the family gathered

around the table, she closed her eyes to give thanks but no words came. In the silence God whispered to her heart 'What God has cleansed, call thou not unclean'. What a rebuke! God had not only cleansed the woman from her sins but also from her leprosy. What right had Anne to think and act in such an ungracious manner?

Aloud she asked God to forgive her and gave thanks for the meal He had provided. She ate all that was on her plate and never again did she find that particular dish so distasteful.

Arriving home one night towards the end of November, Anne realised that something was wrong. A group of neighbours were gathered on her doorstep and they all began to talk at the same time, anxious to tell her what had happened.

'Suriadi very sick.' 'He vomit much blood.' 'Tutik take him to the hospital.' And inside the house bloodstained sheets confirmed their story.

By the time Anne reached the hospital haemorrhagic fever had been diagnosed and she knew that in his poor physical condition the chances of recovery were almost nil. As Anne faced death in this little boy she realised how emotionally involved she had become with her children, especially Suriadi, who had

57

suffered so much in his short life.

Faithfully Tutik remained at his bedside feeding him with glucose at fifteen minute intervals. Indonesian hospitals provide food, treatment and drugs but the provision of bedding and nursing care are the responsibility of the patient's family. Nurses often refuse to stay alone on the wards at night, fearful of the evil spirits which they believe lurk in the darkness. Instead they turn down the drips and retire with their colleagues to sleep until daylight.

The moment of crisis passed and miraculously Suriadi began to recover. Although suffering from malnutrition and hydrocephalus this little boy of just four-and-a-half years had now fought and won a battle against haemorrhagic fever. His determination and will to survive were truly amazing and gradually he regained strength and was able to go home. During December he began to crawl across the floor and Anne and Tutik marvelled at all the hurdles he had overcome. Truly God in His love and mercy was watching over him.

Christmas 1975 was to remain for Anne one of her special memories and the first spent with her Beth Shan family.

They had been invited to spend the day with

Pontas and Mavis and at six o'clock in the morning they set out by becak (pedicab) for the Bible School. Anne was greeted with a breakfast of bacon and eggs which was a wonderful surprise and a great treat. Later they exchanged gifts and sat and shared together, remembering how two thousand years earlier, into a world that had no room for Him, another Baby was born.

As the year drew to a close, in the quietness of her heart Anne looked back. Adi was now almost six months old and a fine, healthy boy. Suriadi was still terrified when approached by strangers and far from strong but he was gaining ground. Munarsih, known affectionately to the family as 'Snoos', was settled and happy although very small for her age.

The village folk were involved, too, with as many as a hundred squeezing into Beth Shan for the monthly fellowship meeting.

Ahead lay another year and beside her would be the same, great God.

5

1976 – 1978

The family grows. Land to build on.

Four more children arrived to join the Beth Shan family during January 1976. First came two delightful little Chinese boys from West Java who were brought to Anne by their widowed mother. She had struggled desperately to provide for Cap Sen, aged three, and two-year-old Li Sen, but it was an impossible task. When she heard of an orphanage in Baron she decided to come and see for herself.

She recognised at once that Beth Shan would offer her children opportunities that she could never give them and the following day, with a heavy heart, she returned to West Java alone.

For two days the little boys were inconsolable, pleading through their tears to be taken back to their mother and their home. They were totally confused by this sudden traumatic change in their lives and could not understand why their mother had abandoned them. Tutik found their grief devastating to watch.

Gently Anne persevered in her efforts to befriend them. 'My name is Ibu' she told them over and over again. 'I love you and Jesus loves you. I want you to be happy here'. Cap Sen looked at her for the first time. 'Your name is Mami', he declared, 'not Ibu'. From that day Anne was to be 'Mami' to every member of the Beth Shan family.

A few days later two more Chinese children, Yanto and Lidia, arrived. They were totally deaf from birth although there was no history of deafness on either side of the family. Yanto was four years old and Lidia two.

With the birth of a second deaf child the father had walked out and the marriage ended in divorce. There were clearly strong bonds between the mother and her children but with no-one to care for them she was unable to work and with the superstition that surrounded deafness her family refused to help.

At first the children were deeply upset and ate very little. They wanted their mother and, like Cap Sen and Li Sen, they could not understand why their lives had suddenly changed so drastically.

The crying of deaf children is loud and disturbing and the communication barrier made it difficult to quieten and comfort them, but the Beth Shan family was eager to show that they loved and cared and slowly the children began to adapt to the routine of their new life.

The growing number of children gradually learnt to love and accept one another and discovered that playing together was fun, in spite of the occasional squabbles and fights.

Suriadi was determined to join in the fun and with his body now less swollen he was able to crawl further. The other children were discouraged from helping him too much and slowly he learnt to make his own contribution to the life of the family.

Anne introduced daily prayers with a short Bible story and this served to deepen the bonds that were being forged between them.

On a dull and dismal day in February Anne alighted from a becak at the gate of Beth Shan, carrying in her arms an exhausted three-and-a-half year old boy. She had just collected him from the Bible School and he was fast asleep.

He had made the long and tedious journey from his home in Kalimantan (Borneo), travelling by sea to Surabaya and then on to Solo by land. He was in the care of two students from his area who were shortly to enrol in Pontas' Bible School.

His name was Sabdinator, shortened to Sab, and he was a member of the Dyak tribe.

He was the only surviving child of a family of nine children, with a background of extreme poverty, and recent flooding had ruined his father's crops. When the local pastor approached the Yayasan for help they agreed at once that he should be offered a home at Beth Shan. Without help he was unlikely to survive to adulthood, living as he was on a diet of green bananas and cassava. He was an emaciated child with serious breathing problems and little energy, and within days of his arrival he had deteriorated further. Anne nursed him at home at first, but when he developed a slight cough she was seriously concerned for him. Following a doctor's examination he was quickly admitted to hospital where tests confirmed that he was suffering from malnutrition and tuberculosis.

Towards the end of April Sab was pronounced well enough to return to Beth Shan although he was still very weak and was confined to bed for a further three months.

As he made progress his cot was moved outside during the day so that he could see all that was going on around him and watch the other children at play.

Anne had now succumbed to a nasty cough

herself, and following tests at the Baptist Hospital in Kediri, tuberculosis was diagnosed and she was admitted as a patient.

Fortunately prompt action had nipped the disease in the bud and within a fortnight she was discharged with the advice that she should have at least two months of complete rest.

To her great relief the doctor stipulated that she should go to 'anywhere except England', thus removing from her the niggling fear that she might be sent home. After a week in Bali and a two month stay in Tawangmangu she returned to Beth Shan rested and refreshed. She resolved to be more disciplined and to curtail unnecessary activities, but with insufficient staff and several sick children it proved difficult to maintain. Becak rides to the doctor, injections, and regular doses of medicine all became part of the Beth Shan routine.

Slowly Sab continued to improve but was still confined to his cot. The frustration of watching the other children play but not being able to join them caused him to become very aggressive.

One August day with only the slightest breeze blowing through the coconut palms the heat was intense. Sab was now well enough to leave his cot for a limited period each day and was overjoyed at the prospect of playing with the other children. Restricting his activity, Anne realised, was not going to be an easy task!

Tutik had called the children in for their lunch and it was not until they were all seated at the table that she realised that someone was missing. Where was Sab? They called and searched without success. Sab had disappeared! Suddenly hearing a mischievous giggle, Anne looked up and spotted a triumphant little boy high up in the papaya tree! She was horrified for he was not yet four years old but when he was retrieved she could not bring herself to punish him. To see his face lit up with the pleasure of doing normal things was a joy beyond words.

Two days later, during a 'cuddle time' with Anne, he shared confidentially, 'Mami, I think that Jesus has made me better so I can climb trees!' It was deeply moving to recognise the stirring of spiritual understanding in such a small boy. He developed a great love for living creatures and would spend long, fascinated moments observing the behaviour of a praying mantis or a grasshopper.

Aniek, Tutik's friend, was now a helper; Pak Timan joined the staff as a gardener and handyman; and an Ibu was employed to help in the house and to cook. Anne and Tutik were relieved to have some of the pressures eased for there were days when there was hardly time to pause for breath!

Agus arrived at the end of July aged just three days. His mother was a cripple and a widow, her husband having been killed in a bus crash just before the baby's birth.

Although she was not able to care for Agus, she was adamant that she did not want him adopted, but finally she changed her mind and agreed that his name should be put forward for adoption. When she left Beth Shan she was never heard of again.

Next came Yokin, a five-month-old child whose mother was mentally disturbed; followed by Yogi, who was two months old and illegitimate and expressed his misery by screaming, crying or just grizzling! The intermittent periods of quiet during the night hours now seemed lost for ever!

By the end of 1976 there was little space left at Beth Shan, with the corridors converted into dormitories at night and the floor covered with sleeping children. Beth Shan was bursting at the seams! Something would have to be done!

Early in May Anne's parents came for a two month visit and she was delighted to have them and to introduce them to her growing family. In spite of the humidity and the mosquitos they enjoyed their stay and returned home at the end of June with a much clearer picture of how Beth Shan was developing. Anne was able to join them on a five-day visit to Bali which proved a very special time.

After being on the staff for two years Aniek had to return home to care for her ageing parents. It was a sad day for all the family and she was greatly missed.

In May ten-year-old Li Min, sister of Cap Sen and Li Sen joined the family. Already a committed Christian she was a joy to have around and the little ones adored her.

With recent changes in government legislation the purchase of land on which to build was now a priority concern. The Department of Social Welfare had already expressed their unwillingness to give a permit for the orphanage in the present premises due to the lack of space and possible health hazards. Their message to Pontas was either to find a larger property or build one! At a meeting of the Yayasan Anne was urged to consider buying a piece of land and to bear in mind the possible need for expansion at a later date.

Land which seemed ideal was discovered on the outskirts of Cemani village just fifteen minutes' walk from the present Beth Shan. It covered an area of 2635 square metres with a road running across it on three sides. It had previously been a rice paddy and sugar plantation and was laid out at three terraced levels, so first the land would have to be levelled as a protection against flooding. Documents would be required to alter the description of the land from rice paddy to building property, a process that would probably take nine months to complete and would also involve a tax payment of 200 rupiahs per square metre. The cost of land at this time was the equivalent of 40 pence per metre in English money. Anne and her staff began to pray, asking God for a large gift of money as confirmation that He wanted them to go ahead.

A Swiss businessman, totally unaware of this possible development, sent Anne a gift of two thousand American dollars! The money was intended for the ongoing support of the work at Beth Shan and was to be used in any way that Anne thought appropriate. She was overwhelmed by this very clear seal of God's approval and blessing. Only a small amount of money was now needed to make the land purchase possible.

On Sunday afternoons Anne and the children now had a new routine, setting out along the road which led to the site, and taking with them biscuits and water to enjoy a picnic when they arrived. Before returning home they always prayed together, asking God specifically for the bricks that would be needed to build their new home. Slowly the building programme got under way and all sorts of gifts began to arrive – money, bricks, cement and even furniture! In Beth Shan a great feeling of excitement and anticipation prevailed.

Bambang, local pastor and member of the Yayasan, was in great need. With the contract time on the house in which he and his family were living running out, the possibility of homelessness loomed large. What about the little house in Baron which before long would become vacant? A couple of extra rooms had been built in the garden for sleeping purposes and in return the landlord had extended the contract to cover a further six months without rent charges. This would give Bambang time and space to find a more permanent home and when Anne offered it to him he accepted with a thankful heart.

At this time Anne was herself being tested with serious cash flow problems. With very little financial support coming in it was difficult to cover even the basic daily needs of her large family and there was nothing at all available to meet any additional building costs. As feelings of panic and despair threatened to overwhelm her she decided to go for a walk so that alone she could pour out her needs and her feelings to God. Her walk led her to the home of a missionary friend and she decided to call in for a chat and to ask for her prayer support. 100,000 rupiahs was needed to pay the workmen and at present the funds were not enough to meet that commitment. Further cash was also needed to cover medical costs and food expenses. Why did God take so long to answer? Did He really supply every need? The questions chased one another round in her mind. It was a great relief to be able to share the burden with a friend and for them to have the opportunity to pray together.

Anne was a firm believer in tithing and had applied this principle to Beth Shan from its earliest days, with one tenth of everything she was given set aside as God's portion, be it cash, rice or clothing. It was a Scriptural principle to which she attached great importance, and only once, under severe financial testing, had she withheld her tithe. Although she had promised on that occasion that she would repay the amount as soon as her finances improved she knew in her heart that this was wrong and soon became aware of God's blessing withheld in spiritual as well as practical matters.

With tears she sought His forgiveness, paid the outstanding tithe, and found her inner peace restored. It was a lesson she vowed never to forget.

Prayer was urgently needed at a national level, too. With the presidential elections drawing near there were many clampdowns by local governments throughout Indonesia and Anne's friends and supporters were praying that she, and others in a similar position, would not be curtailed in their work for the Lord.

A spirit of fear and unrest was abroad and few permits were now being granted for any form of public meeting or campaign. In East Java church meetings held in homes were now forbidden, but as yet Central Java was not affected. There was much prayer for the local government in Solo, that those in authority would find the Christians worthy of their trust and would not fear them as possible instigators of any form of uprising. Many local leaders stopped attending church lest they be arrested for participating in group meetings. These were uneasy times for non-nationals and for Christians in particular.

By the end of 1977 the building of the new Beth Shan was going ahead at a remarkable rate, with specific needs being met as they were brought before the Lord in prayer. There were now seventeen children in the Beth Shan family; ten boys and seven girls. 1978 was going to be an exciting year – of that Anne had no doubt!

6

1978 – 1980

Moving In. Endang arrives.
Another building project.

On March 10th, 1978 the family moved into
their new home. Although the building work
was still not completed it was sufficiently
advanced to make the move possible. What
excitement! At last Anne and her family would
have more space! What luxury! More room to
cook, to sleep, to wash – and just simply 'to
be'!

With insufficient staff and several sick
babies it was not easy to maintain structure and
routine. Adding to the pressures Anne was
teaching Child Care and Health and Hygiene
to the Bible School students, and exhaustion
was beginning to take its toll.

The official opening was just days away
when Bambang offered her a lift back to Beth
Shan. She welcomed the opportunity to talk
with him and to mention her tiredness and the
headaches that were now becoming more
frequent.

'I'd love my parents to see the new Beth Shan,' she told him as he dropped her off. 'Maybe they will be able to come out next year. After all, they're not getting any younger and I have a feeling that my father may not be with me much longer'.

The following day Anne went to Solo Airport to meet Bill McIlroy, her pastor at West Kilburn Baptist Church. He had come to visit for a few weeks and to share with the family in the official opening celebrations. As Anne talked with him on the drive back to Beth Shan she found herself repeating again the feelings she had expressed earlier to Bambang about her father. She was weeping as she spoke. Could this simply be a reaction to the tiredness she was feeling?

Bill listened to her in silence before handing her a letter. It was from her uncle to let her know that following a massive heart attack her father had died. With the opening of Beth Shan so close, the family had felt it wiser not to tell her until the funeral was over. He explained that, knowing Bill was already booked on a flight to Solo to visit her, they had decided to ask him to deliver the letter. It had all happened very suddenly and her uncle was writing immediately after the family's return from the funeral.

The letter was kind and sensitively written, but Anne was devastated. She was angry that no-one had been in touch with her to let her know what had happened and she was angry with God. She had come to Indonesia in obedience to His call and had sought to honour Him in all things. Surely she did not deserve this?

Coming as it did so unexpectedly the news of her father's death was spiritually the last straw and her faith wavered alarmingly. Later she would realise that we cannot present ourselves to God on our own terms; only on His.

Mechanically she went through the final preparations for the official opening of Beth Shan but for the moment her spark and her vision had deserted her.

She learnt that her father would have been a permanent invalid had he lived, but even knowing how much he would have hated that did nothing to lessen her anger and hurt.

Why had she not been notified? Why did she not have the opportunity to fly home for the funeral? The decision had clearly been made in her own best interests with the official opening of Beth Shan so shortly to take place, but she could not accept it.

In September her mother was involved in a

car accident and Anne arranged to fly home on a three-month furlough. Returning home would be a painful experience, knowing that her father would not be there to welcome her, but she knew that her mother needed her.

Together they visited the family in Cornwall before returning to Leicester where her parents had made their home in recent years. She was aware of her mother's deep emotional needs but with her own feelings in disarray she felt able to do little to help.

In November Anne received a letter from Beth Shan which jolted her thinking back into focus. As she read of new laws and consequent instability in Indonesia she struggled to calm her thoughts and control her fears.

What of her future? How would these latest changes affect her? She realised that it was essential to work towards making Beth Shan self-supporting. In prayer times with friends she felt strengthened and encouraged and in the midst of all her turmoil she knew that God's hand was upon her life and upon the future of Beth Shan. One fear that constantly raised its head was that she might be asked to leave the country, and repeatedly she had to remind herself that the ultimate responsibility rested with God and not with her.

Her part was to obey and to follow without

questioning His ways, for He alone 'does all things well'.

She returned to Java on December 3rd, taking her mother with her. During the flight she pondered on the many wonderful ways in which God had proved His love and faithfulness to her since her first arrival in the country in 1972. How could she fail to trust Him for the future, whatever it might hold?

Arriving at Jakarta early on Sunday morning they were able to catch an internal flight to Solo the same day. But as they neared Solo Airport the plane was redirected to Semarang and once again panic gripped her heart. Further delay was frustrating and getting home would now involve expensive taxi fares which she could not afford. How slow she was to learn God's lessons! He was soon to remind her again that He truly does have all things under control. A Chinese businessman invited Anne and her mother to share his taxi, refused any contribution towards the fare, and instructed the driver to drop them off at the gates of Beth Shan!

Now that she was back again with her family Anne's spirits began to rise. Adi surveyed her with eyes that were apprehensive and questioning. 'Mami. How could you leave me for such a long time? Will you leave me again tomorrow?' His eyes asked the questions for which he was too small to have words, but before many days had passed Anne was thankful as she saw his trust in her returning.

Settling back into routine was not easy especially with her mother's deep emotional needs never far from her thoughts, but day by day God gave the patience and wisdom that life at Beth Shan continued to demand.

Christmas Day dawned and as Anne sat opposite her mother to share a special Christmas breakfast the tears fell freely. So much had happened in a short space of time and the first Christmas without a dearly loved husband and father was bound to be painful.

New Year's Eve passed quietly. What would the coming year hold? Anne had no idea but she did know that God would remain faithful and sufficient for all her needs.

The night watchman was not at all happy. He insisted that he needed decent accommodation and not the building intended for a chicken-house, but Anne was adamant – it was that or nothing!

Pak Timan was Beth Shan's maintenance man, and when he heard about the argument he quickly sought Anne out. Sugiati, his wife, had now also joined the staff and they were in desperate need of somewhere to live. Would

Anne allow him to convert the chicken-house and the storeroom attached to it into a home for his family? Anne agreed willingly and Pak Timan was delighted, setting to work without delay and with great enthusiasm. Gradually he produced a more than adequate family dwelling and when he and Sugiati moved in with their two-year-old son there was great rejoicing.

It was good to feel more secure and to be more closely involved in the daily life of Beth Shan. Meanwhile a disgruntled night watchman slept on a rush mat outside the kitchen door!

It was the afternoon of April 1st, 1979 when Endang arrived at Beth Shan and as Anne watched her arrival with Pontas and a local doctor her heart sank. How could she possibly love THAT? Endang was fourteen years old and a street tramp. She had knocked on the door of the doctor's house asking for bread and he had at once contacted Pontas.

Although only the size of an eight-year-old everything about Endang was quite repulsive. Her clothes were filthy and reeked of body odour, her hair was matted and alive, and a fungal infection covered her face.

Her arms displayed a mass of open wounds where in sheer frenzy she had bitten into her own flesh, and her eyes, wild and evil, made her appearance quite alarming.

She had been the victim of cruelty at the hands of her father and stepmother and burn marks, many of them unhealed, bore testimony to some of the suffering she had endured. Finally, in desperation she had fled to a new life on the streets of Solo.

She looked and behaved like a wild animal with unco-ordinated movements over which she had no control. The other children came to look at her then scattered, screaming and afraid.

Endang's early days at Beth Shan were a nightmare and both the children and the staff were petrified when she was near them.

She was totally unpredictable, suddenly going berserk and biting deeply and at random any child near enough to become her victim. All the doors were securely locked by day and night as she watched furtively for any opportunity to escape. Sometimes she would go missing for forty-eight hours at a stretch before she was traced and taken back to Beth Shan, protesting loudly and vigorously all the way.

Anne felt completely out of her depth and decided to set aside one day each week for prayer and fasting, pleading with God for Endang's healing and release.

On those days she would invariably either

run away or have very violent outbursts as a spiritual battle raged. The presence of evil spirits was apparent and those spirits had to be exorcised. Aware of their limited experience in this field Anne and her staff came together regularly to pray about the situation. Any mention of the name of Jesus or the reading aloud of the Scriptures met with an immediate and violent response, but the praying continued.

Gradually however, the staff became aware of a change in Endang. She would sit in on the prayer times and began to join in the singing and the prayers. Her rendering of 'Yes, God is good' may not have been very accurate from a musical point of view but it was certainly music to the ears of those who listened! It was evident that Endang had received a measure of peace, and encouraged by her progress the staff continued to pray for her complete healing and deliverance.

They prayed for her very poor eyesight which had failed to respond to large doses of vitamin A, and because spectacles were so expensive they were out of the question. In any case they would probably have been destroyed within twenty four hours!

She had been doubly incontinent at first but was gradually responding to training. She was promised a bed if she remained dry for seven nights with the promise of a mattress at the end of a further month. It was a slow, uphill struggle but with faith and a sense of humour the progress continued.

It remained essential to watch her, especially during the night hours when she was likely to get up to all sorts of tricks.

On one occasion she managed to get hold of the storeroom keys and had a wonderful time while the rest of the family slept. To her great delight she discovered a box containing forty-eight tins of sardines. This was treasure indeed!

Opening one tin after another she poured the oil over the floor before sampling the contents which she then spat, well chewed, back into the tins! Her enjoyment quickly faded however, when she was discovered and was refused her breakfast until she had cleared up all the mess. Anne gave her a bucket of water, a cloth and a tin of vim and left her to it. This was one battle she could not afford to lose!

Progress continued among the other children, too, with ten of them starting school and looking very proud and smart in their new school uniforms. Anne felt quite emotional as she waved them off to walk the two miles to the village school.

Most of them had overcome serious medical

problems and most had been through deep emotional trauma. Now they were experiencing their first taste of a normal family routine.

Lidia was now five years old and she and her brother Yanto had both been given places at a special school for deaf children. The school was several hours' drive from Solo so they had to go as boarders. The family missed them during term-time but were thrilled to see the progress they had made when they returned home for the long school holidays.

In May Anne and Mavis Pardede were invited to share with other Christian workers and missionaries in a retreat at Bandung and it proved a time of great encouragement and blessing. The theme of the retreat was 'Prayer' and together they discovered many untapped areas and the need to channel energies in the right direction. There was lengthy discussion on the futility of 'busyness' and on the importance of safeguarding time spent alone with God.

Anne returned to Beth Shan determined to put into practice the teaching she had absorbed, but it was to prove a discipline that was far from easy to maintain. Funding at this time was more than sufficient for the immediate needs of her large family and she marvelled at the generous love and faithfulness of God.

On June 2nd, 1980 the Beth Shan family celebrated their fourth Thanksgiving Day, the second in their new building. This year was to be more of a family celebration with just the Yayasan and their wives as guests. For the first time Anne decided to combine with their celebrations a 'giving' day as a 'thank you' to God for all His goodness to them.

Dressed in their best clothes and resplendent with bright ribbons and bows, the children could hardly contain their excitement. They had practised over and over again the songs and choruses they would sing, but with the eyes of so many important guests fixed upon them they were completely over-awed. They stood there, wide-eyed and open-mouthed – but totally silent!

Later, however, feeling more relaxed, they gave of their best as they enacted a jungle story, complete with costumes, and it was a performance that more than compensated for their earlier shaky start.

As Anne rolled into bed very late that night she knew that nothing done for the Lord is ever in vain. The message of the Bandung retreat still burned in her heart but the needs of such a large family and the interruptions and demands which seemed endless continued to thwart her aims and intentions.

There was anxiety, too, as more news filtered through of cancelled visas and further tightening up of regulations which restricted the activities of non-nationals, and among her missionary friends many would be required to leave within the next six months.

Anne knew she was safe until 1980 – but what then? What would become of her children if she was required to leave Indonesia? Would it be in the best interests of the children for her to seek to remain longer? She had no real answers but arranged to meet with Mavis every Tuesday so that together they could make the whole situation a matter of earnest prayer.

On June 25th, a missionary prayer meeting was held at Beth Shan and in spite of so much uncertainty it was a wonderful time of praise and thanksgiving that uplifted the hearts of all who were there. Whatever difficulties lay ahead, God was assuredly building His church in Indonesia.

The timely message of the speaker, John Elliott, went home to every heart. This was God's work, not theirs. Preparation and prayer must be to the end that every project would be able to stand and grow whatever developed in the land. Living on the edge of a precipice need not cause alarm as long as God was leading and His children were faithfully following. Oh, for the faith and courage to follow – whatever the cost.

Meanwhile life at Beth Shan continued with its normal pattern of ups and downs. Endang had taken a great dislike to Suriadi and had to be watched carefully. He still needed a lot of extra attention and care and this annoyed her intensely. She had clearly become very jealous and had to be disciplined again and again.

Aware that she was not very well physically, Anne decided to have a checkup at Kediri Baptist Hospital. The checkup revealed a benign tumour and following successful surgery, having been advised to take a holiday, she left with a missionary friend to stay at Pasir Putih, a little coastal spot in East Java. At a reasonable price they were able to rent a room looking out across the Indian Ocean, an idyllic setting for a much needed break.

For part of their stay they had the complete seafront to themselves and revelled in the sheer bliss of reading, chatting and resting. They walked for miles along the beach, past mangrove swamps where flying fish flitted to safety as soon as they became aware of the presence of humans.

They enjoyed sea trips in search of coral and when the heat became too intense they could just sit and admire the breathtaking scenery. It was a wonderful and uplifting experience, with God so near that they felt they could almost reach out and touch Him.

On her return Anne received an enthusiastic welcome from the family with children jostling one another for a share of her luggage to carry triumphantly indoors. They clamoured for her attention, eager to share with her the special bits of news which they had saved for her return. What a wonderful thing it was to be so loved and to be well enough to enjoy such a rumbustious welcome.

Just three days after her return to Beth Shan however, Anne collapsed, and when she regained consciousness she was in considerable pain.

A missionary friend who was visiting the family took her back to Kediri Hospital where she at once underwent various tests. Lying in bed with plenty of time to think she was angry and disappointed at being re-admitted to hospital so soon.

A couple of days later the doctor visited her. 'You really have got God on your side,' he began. Still feeling very disgruntled Anne asked him what he meant.

'Had you not blacked out,' he told her 'we would never have discovered that you have TB of the spine and this would have resulted eventually in paralysis from the waist down.'

'Yes, God really is on my side'. 'His everlasting arms are underneath me'. 'His banner over me is love'. 'The angel of the Lord encamps around those who fear Him.' One after another, verses of Scripture passed through her mind as she lay in bed, and her anger faded. Lying flat on her back she had plenty of time to think and to pray and determined to use this experience to the best advantage. Above all, she wanted to learn at a deeper level how to relinquish everything into God's hands.

After a three week stay in hospital Anne left for the mountains of Tawangmangu, the area which had been her home when she first arrived in Java in 1972.

On her return to Beth Shan she found herself once again plunged into long and busy days. Especially poignant at this time was the departure of Tutik who was to be married on October 12th.

In her mind Anne relived that evening when Tutik had returned from Madiun carrying in her arms a tiny baby named Adityokrisnuyudha (Adi), the first child to be entrusted to her care. Tutik's future husband was a pastor and after her marriage they would be living on the other side of the town but she had offered to do sewing for the children whenever her time permitted.

The wedding day dawned and the joy and celebration of such a special occasion was to remain one of Anne's treasured memories. Wherever the future might take her, Tutik would always keep her own place within the Beth Shan family.

During her stay in hospital Anne had been visited by the Yayasan. Would she consider admitting to Beth Shan an eleven-month-old baby boy who was blind? With a serious shortage of staff the idea seemed far from wise, but when she learnt that he had been turned away from several other places she knew that she could not refuse to take him.

When Sutrisno arrived it was obvious that blindness was not his only problem. He could not roll or grip and was unable to sit up or move unaided; his body seemed devoid of all spontaneous reactions. Anne arranged for him to be examined at a special clinic, and when the doctors were unable to diagnose his condition an urgent request for prayer was sent out on his behalf.

With thirty-seven children now living at Beth Shan the need for electricity to be brought to the house became a matter of vital importance.

The addition of a water pump and a washing machine would relieve some of the pressures, particularly for Sugiati who still continued to wash by hand for the ever-growing family. She did so without complaint and often came to work on her day off in an effort to keep on top of the work load. When asked how she coped Sugiati's reply was always the same, 'God has done so much for me and I am glad to do this work for Him.' By now she was seven months pregnant with her second child.

The year 1979 ended with the prospect of another exciting building project. Beth Shan had received the wonderful gift of 1,000 square metres of land just half a mile further on in the village, at the place where all the daily vegetables were purchased from a local family. Previously Pontas and Mavis had shared with Anne their vision for a kindergarten school to be built near to Beth Shan, where the village children as well as Beth Shan's toddlers would be catered for. Pontas wanted to see such a school staffed by Christians who would first receive special training at his Bible School. Emphasis would be placed on child evangelism and Christian education to a standard recognised by the Indonesian government and also by the newly formed Department of Religious Affairs.

It was possible that the Bible School would also introduce a more detailed programme in Child Care which would give nationals the opportunity to gain a certificate in this field. This land would be the ideal site for such a school and would present a wonderful opportunity for outreach into the local community.

Pahala, a graduate teacher from the Bible School, was appointed to join the Beth Shan staff and to liaise between the Yayasan and government officers as the project got under way.

During the early weeks of 1980 the building of the kindergarten school went ahead rapidly with the village people monitoring progress as eagerly as Anne and the Yayasan.

It was around this time that Pak Mesdi, Pak Timan's younger brother, came to work at Beth Shan to help with the ever-increasing amount of maintenance work. Although he was a Muslim he would often attend staff prayers and after a time he became a Christian. He went home to his village to share his new-found faith with his wife and she also became a Christian.

The Yayasan asked Pak Mesdi to build a

little house close to the kindergarten school and to enquire around for someone suitable to live there as night watchman. When the house was completed Pak Mesdi asked the Yayasan if he could take on the job himself, providing at the same time a home for his wife and five children. The couple were delighted when the Yayasan agreed.

7

1980 – 1982

Kindergarten school. A Toyota Pick-up.
Floods and drought.

On June 2nd, the kindergarten school was officially dedicated with village folk arriving from far and near to join in the celebrations. Children from the village sat and played alongside the Beth Shan toddlers and the teachers, fresh from Pontas' Bible School, were thrilled to be on the staff. Pak and Ibu Mesdi and their family moved into their new home with Pak Mesdi now responsible for the maintenance of the kindergarten school premises, while Ibu Mesdi was appointed cook to the Beth Shan family. It was a day of great celebration.

In early August Anne returned to England on furlough, desperate for a rest and the opportunity to lay down for a while the great burden of responsibility that she carried. With confidence she left Sugiati in charge, with the support of Warni, another staff member, knowing that the Yayasan would be at hand should any crisis arise during her absence.

To spend time with her family and friends and to share with them in more detail about the work at Beth Shan; to enjoy church worship in her own language; to walk in the autumn sunshine and to marvel at the ever-changing colours of the leaves in a riot of orange, brown and gold – these were all such precious experiences, but when October 21st arrived and her plane took off for Jakarta it was even more thrilling to know that she was returning to the family and home specially given to her by God. This was now where she truly belonged.

On arriving back at Beth Shan it was a great shock to discover that Sugiati had contracted primary tuberculosis, and although she was responding well to treatment, she was clearly very tired and discouraged. For her husband Timan and their two little boys it was a difficult time.

Anne received a further shock when she saw the deterioration in Suriadi's health. By the time he was nine years old his legs had grown stronger, he had started to talk, and to the great delight of all the family he had started to attend the kindergarten school. During August, however, while Anne was on furlough, his condition had begun to give cause for concern.

He was losing weight and had undergone two operations to drain an infection behind his ear. As Anne sat on his bed to talk to him she was alarmed to see how tired and emaciated he looked and how sunken his eyes were. She noticed a piece of paper peeping out from under his pillow; it was the last letter she had written to him before her return from England.

During Anne's absence Shirabinatum had joined the family. She was just one week old when she arrived and had a large, ugly growth between her eyes and down her nose. Her mother had died in childbirth and when her father saw her condition he had abandoned her. She was now three months old and as she grew the protrusion grew too, making medical help now a matter of urgency.

At that time there were only two hospitals in Indonesia equipped to cope with the major brain surgery that would be required and one of them was in Jakarta.

With Suriadi needing a further operation for mastoiditis Anne decided to leave for Jakarta taking both children with her. A flight was booked for November 2nd, 1980.

Christine Matthews, who was the wife of a Christian businessman in Jakarta, lived quite near the hospital and she offered Anne accommodation for as long as she needed it. She was at the airport to meet Anne when she arrived and took her and the two children straight away to the hospital.

Following a thorough examination the surgeon agreed to admit Shirabinatum at once but said that Suriadi was too weak to undergo surgery; he would need to wait a further week while efforts were made to build him up.

Injections were prescribed to fight the infection and drugs to stimulate his appetite, and taking Suriadi with her Anne moved into the Matthews' home. He needed constant nursing care but with Christine's home helper available to cover night care for Shirabinatum Anne was able to get some rest and sleep.

Each day she took Suriadi to the hospital for his injections and took care of Shirabinatum as she lay in her cot. A lung infection caused a further month's delay before she was well enough to have the operation.

On the Sunday night Suriadi developed a high fever and became delirious and by Monday he just wanted to sleep and was difficult to rouse.

Getting him to take liquids was now a problem as he would just shake his head and fall again into a deep sleep. An examination revealed a thrombosis behind his eye and he was clearly getting weaker. When spells of vomiting developed he was admitted to hospital and a lumbar puncture was performed.

Further complications developed and Anne realised that it would now take a miracle to save his life. When the ear infection spread to the back of the brain and to the spine meningitis developed and by three o'clock that afternoon he was fighting for his life. At six o'clock Anne was persuaded to go home and get some rest, with the promise that she would be kept informed of Suriadi's condition. In the comfort of Christine's home she relaxed in a warm bath and once the evening meal was over decided to go to bed. She was exhausted.

She had just settled into bed when the telephone rang. Suriadi was going downhill fast and she should come at once. When she arrived at the hospital it was already too late; Suriadi was dead. It was just four days after his tenth birthday.

Collecting the death certificate and a letter from the doctors for the Yayasan, Anne and Christine returned home, both of them in a state of shock.

Endless questions chased one another through Anne's mind. After all he had come through, all he had achieved, why did God let him die? She remembered the times when tiredness had made her impatient with him; and she wept. Finally, broken, confused and unable to pray she fell into bed and slept.

Early the next morning she went out into the garden, and in the quietness poured out her heart to the Lord. 'Be still and know that I am God'. As the words of a familiar song came into her mind she knew that God was speaking to her. 'Stop struggling. Stop trying to work things out. I am God, your God'. As she listened God gave her a new verse to the song and she could almost hear the music. 'My ways in you are ways of love'.

Suriadi was buried the next day on the outskirts of Jakarta.

Anne remained for several more days, visiting Shirabinatum and caring for her throughout the day. Her condition was very serious and there was only a slight hope that she would come through the operation. In spite of all her inner turmoil and her grief over Suriadi's death Anne knew that God could save the little girl's life.

On Friday Anne returned to Beth Shan taking Shirabinatum with her. She had survived the operation, the growth had been removed, and a metal plate fitted.

As sensitively as she could Anne told the children of Suriadi's death. It was not an easy task as the children asked many questions and shed a lot of tears.

Endang in particular was inconsolable. For

months she had been jealous of Suriadi, sometimes to the point of cruelty, but during his illness her attitude had changed and she had become attentive and kind, feeding him and loving him, where before she would have been hitting him and trying to knock him off balance. For a long time she remained confused and sad. Later Anne would see how God can bring blessings out of apparent tragedies.

Elisa aged five and her three-year-old sister Desianti were among the new arrivals towards the end of the year. Their father had died and their mother could not afford to keep them. By the end of 1980 sixty-one children had found refuge at Beth Shan including several who were later adopted and happily settled with their new families. Menik, who lived locally, had now joined the staff and together with Pak Timan and Pak Mesdi Anne now had seven helpers.

Beth Shan, a place of refuge, was proving to be an ever-expanding vision.

During May 1981 there was again much activity, as another house was built close to the home of Pak and Ibu Timan. It was to be the home of Mr. and Mrs. Poniman and their two children, who were travelling from East Java to join the Beth Shan staff. Mr. Poniman was appointed to help with administration while his wife, who was an auxiliary nurse, would divide her time between Beth Shan and the kindergarten school.

Anne had long been praying for a couple to support her in the work and she looked forward eagerly to their arrival in July.

Shirabinatum was again very unwell. The operation she had undergone in Jakarta had failed to remove the root of the growth and within a couple of months it had started to grow again. She began to have fits brought on by the slightest exertion and an examination revealed that she had water on the brain. In spite of all her health problems, however, she was adopted in July by a German couple who had been taking a special interest in her. They renamed her Julia.

In Germany, on August 12th, Julia underwent major facial surgery and during her seven hours in the operating theatre surgeons discovered that she had no nasal bones. A couple of days later Anne received a message to let her know that although she was still in intensive care the little girl was making satisfactory progress.

Endang was now seventeen years old and there was a marked improvement in her behaviour. She had learnt to pray and to express herself in her own words, and she loved to sing. At full moon she was given permission to sleep out of doors with the other children and could scarcely contain her excitement, but she remained unpredictable and there were still unexpected setbacks.

It was three o'clock in the afternoon and Endang, feeling restless, was longing for the freedom of her old life on the streets of Solo.

She remembered the cement drainage pipe that had provided an escape route in the past and stealthily she set off. As she began to crawl through the pipe she was soon in trouble, having put on quite a lot of weight since she last made use of this particular exit, and halfway along she got stuck! She tried to crawl backwards to the entrance but she could not move. She was well and truly stuck!

When Anne and the other searchers found her they knew that they had a major task ahead of them. They tried to release Endang's arm which was now firmly wedged across the pipe but had to abandon the idea fearing that her arm might get broken.

Desperate situations often call for desperate measures and finally, having dosed her with pheno-barbitone, Anne threw buckets of water into the pipe and smeared cream soap all over the sides. To ensure a smooth exit she plastered Endang with cream soap as well!

By now a small crowd had gathered and were totally enthralled as Anne wrapped towels round Endang's legs and with the help of a couple of men from the village finally pulled her out!

Anne was so relieved by her safe exit that she began to pray aloud, thanking God for His help. Endang was obviously relieved too, as she flung herself at Anne in a huge embrace. Anne felt hopeless as she stood there, covered with pale blue soap and all the other things that make up the contents of an Indonesian ditch!

Endang had the knack of forgetting the problems of yesterday very quickly once a new day had dawned, and five days later anyone who happened to be around at three o'clock in the morning would have caught a glimpse of Anne transporting Endang back to Beth Shan on the back of her bicycle.

Anang was another runaway, but he was proving more difficult to trace. Twenty-four hours had elapsed before he was discovered at the home of his grandmother, a journey of three-and-a-half hours by car from Beth Shan. He had previously spent three days at home over a Muslim holiday and during that time had been subjected to abuse and insulting behaviour. His mother had married a man whom Anang disliked intensely and the couple had then left for another island without informing him of their intentions. It was an act of gross rejection and Anang could not cope with it. Back at Beth Shan he sat on Anne's lap and wept with all the grief of a rejected child.

His three sisters had also been cared for at Beth Shan until they were adopted into the home of a German couple and it all seemed so unfair! They now had a mum and dad who loved them but he had been considered too old for adoption and the pain of such total rejection was almost too great to bear.

In July the Poniman family arrived and were pleased with the newly built home provided for them and the two children quickly settled into their new school. All seemed well at first but gradually problems began to creep in and Anne had an uneasy feeling about the level of their commitment.

In spite of all that had been discussed during their interview with the Yayasan they were only prepared to work set hours, reserving the remainder of the time for their own family life. They made it clear that apart from their working hours they did not want to be involved in the life of the Beth Shan family and did not like to be disturbed once their days' work was done. It was obvious that they could not measure up to the demands of such a busy life and in mid-September they resigned.

This decision came as a great blow to Anne, having listened to them as they shared their testimony of how God had guided them and called them to join her in the work at Beth Shan. At a meeting with the Yayasan they acknowledged that they were finding the work too hard and the demands upon their time too great.

Although the departure of the Ponimans added to the work load of an already overstretched staff the daily routine settled down again surprisingly quickly.

The arrival of two Bible School students to gain six months practical experience in Child Care confirmed how perfect God's timing always is as Dorce and Hermina threw themselves wholeheartedly into the family life of Beth Shan.

Early in December Audrey Corser arrived to stay for a few months and Anne was glad to have her company. Audrey, who had spent several years in Africa and was a trained nurse, quickly established her own special place within the life of the family as staff and children alike responded to her kindness and love.

Her name was not easy for an Indonesian child to pronounce and she soon became 'Tante Emi'.

Over the 1981 Christmas celebrations a total of four hundred and twenty-two visitors had come and gone and consequently the New Year began with a backlog of jobs that had accumulated over the Christmas period.

Early in the New Year extensive flooding caused serious problems as the river rose nine feet before overflowing its banks. Several homes in the village were completely washed away and others were seriously damaged. Two villagers were drowned, and Beth Shan temporarily became a place of refuge for a number of village people who lived nearby. With the river serving also as the village loo the stench was awful and in Beth Shan itself every room was flooded to a depth of between six and twelve inches.

The children rallied to the cause and worked very hard during the extensive 'mopping up' operations.

Not only did the waters rise but with the roof of Beth Shan leaking in so many places it became clear that the building would need complete re-roofing.

With torrential rain and no sunshine the drying of nappies became a nightmare, especially when an outbreak of diarrhoea affected the five babies and eight toddlers.

Anne became quite skilled at drying nappies with the aid of three electric fans and an electric oven!

Whenever she paused to look back over the years since the vision of Beth Shan had become a reality Anne could not fail to marvel at the miracles of God's provision for her large family and at His undertaking at every time of crisis. Once again, however, shortage of funds was causing her some anxiety and although she knew it was wrong to be anxious she acknowledged her constant concern in the areas of finance. Medical care was very expensive and with so many children needing special attention the costs were alarming. One visit to the doctor would cost £2.50 in English money, an amount which represented a large part of the average weekly wage of most village workers. How thankful she was for a Christian doctor who made herself available to Beth Shan without charging for her services. In recent months inadequate X-ray readings had resulted in thirteen children being incorrectly diagnosed as having tuberculosis and treated accordingly.

In addition Agus, aged five, was found to have a heart murmur and one-year-old Daud had congenital heart disease.

Anang had undergone surgery to remove a tumour from the roof of his mouth at a cost of

129,000 rupiahs (£43) with a further £32 for post operative medicines. Thankfully Anang's tumour had proved to be non-malignant and he now seemed more settled.

An outbreak of flu left many of the children with nasty coughs and Audrey Corser's help and support was invaluable. Her care of the children was outstanding and her ability to cope with the inevitable office work was a great relief to Anne.

Endang continued to make good progress and enjoyed being allowed to help with the little ones, sitting them on their potties and straightening up their cots before they were settled down for the night.

Anne developed a special concern for Agus at this time. He had been considered for adoption but it was necessary to first obtain his mother's permission and all efforts to trace her had failed. With heart disease now confirmed what would his future hold? It was with children like Agus in mind that Anne began to seriously consider the possibility of becoming an Indonesian citizen. The process was long and complicated and was liable to change at the drop of a hat, but it continued to be an issue that dominated her thoughts.

From time to time Anne received further news of Julia (Shirabinatum) and was thrilled to learn that she was continuing to gain strength and was reaping the benefits of the massive surgery she had undergone.

Okok, who had come to Beth Shan as an unwanted baby, was now a year old. Efforts by his mother to abort him had resulted in brain damage and poor co-ordination, but he defied the medical prognosis as he developed into an energetic and mischievous little boy.

Audrey was so much enjoying her time at Beth Shan that she decided to apply for a three month extension on her visa. All the family, and Anne in particular, were as thrilled as Audrey herself when permission was granted.

Anne was relieved that her own visa was extended to March 1983 and she continued to work on the papers concerning her application for Indonesian citizenship.

Andik was fourteen months old when he arrived at Beth Shan. He was seriously underweight and malnourished and was so weak that he required feeding at half-hourly intervals both day and night. He was eighteen months old before he was able to sit up and well over two years before he started to walk. His mother had recently remarried, and when she expressed her wish to reclaim the child it was agreed that he would return to her in October when his treatment for tuberculosis was completed. When a sick child has needed constant nursing care the bond that develops is strong and Anne was dreading the day when she must part with him.

He was much too young to understand the Scriptures and she prayed that there would be an opportunity to reach his mother for God.

Around this time another family of three children also left Beth Shan having lived with Anne for five years. Their father had been killed in a military accident and as their mother was one of eighteen children there had been no room for them all to move in with the grandmother. Now, with the mother trained and rehabilitated she was able to take her children home. One of them, nine-year-old Prabowo, had been presented with a Bible as a prize when he learnt by heart the whole of Psalm 119 – no mean feat for such a young child! On the day of their departure the two little girls were given illustrated Bibles and the mother also accepted a copy.

It was a tearful time of farewell for everyone, but Anne prayed that the Word of God would become living and real for each member of that little family.

Early in July Pak and Ibu Mesdi testified to their Christian faith through baptism and it was a time of great rejoicing. Two of their children had remained in their home village where they were living with Muslim relatives, and special prayers were said for them during the service.

Java was experiencing a period of extreme drought and there appeared to be no prospect of rain in the near future. The cocoa and coffee crops were dying and would take years to replace. How far away the torrential rains of January now seemed!

Somehow Anne managed to bathe her large family with just one bucket of water. One small scoop to wet, followed by a soaping, with the next child stepping into the used water of the first, and so on, with each child receiving another small scoop to rinse themselves. After all, this was really quite a hygienic arrangement compared with bathing in the local river which also served as the village loo!

As the situation became more serious the washing had to be taken to another well, and the children had to take their baths elsewhere. Carrying heavy buckets of water was back breaking work!

As a result of the damage done in the January floods Beth Shan now had a new roof, and the family praised God for providing the necessary finance and for protecting the workmen from any injury. Baby Adityo, after just a brief stay, was adopted by an English couple living in Yogyakarta. His adoptive father was working as an engineering advisor to the Indonesian government on irrigation projects and the couple were delighted to welcome a new young life into their home.

A volcanic eruption in West Java caused panic and fear among the Sudanese people. 'Why is God angry with us?' 'What have we done?' As a result, when a converted Muslim travelled around preaching the gospel eighteen villages turned to Christ. £6,000 was collected to purchase Bibles, but with insufficient copies available many converts had to wait a long time before they could have one of their own.

Danang was accidentally dropped by his sister when he was five months old and as a result he was severely epileptic, sometimes suffering as many as thirty fits in a day. He was nine months old when his parents brought him to Beth Shan.

They were poor and in desperate need with several other children to care and provide for. The father was a pedicab driver with very little money coming in and there was hardly any surplus cash available to cover Danang's medical needs.

Already they had sold their furniture and now, with nothing else left to sell, they confessed that in their desperation they had prayed for their child to die. Could Anne take him in and look after him for a while? The Yayasan agreed that he could come to Beth Shan for three months – and his parents wept with relief.

On a day in early December Anne responded to loud knocking at the door of Beth Shan. 'You don't know me', said the lady standing there 'but we have heard about your work and have brought you a gift.' She handed Anne a book displaying on the front a Toyota Kijang pick-up! It had been built like a van, with canvas sides, and would be suitable for transporting either children or goods. Anne struggled to find suitable words of thanks but she was totally overwhelmed!

Shortly before Christmas, with the promised vehicle due to be delivered at any time, a group of welfare officials arrived at Beth Shan. They had come to bring Christmas greetings and a gift of rice and asked Anne if they could be shown round the orphanage. When they reached the room where Danang was sitting in his chair Anne noticed that he was unusually quiet and had a strange look in his eyes.

Expressing her concern to her visitors she went across to look at him more closely. 'As soon as these people have gone,' she thought, 'I will take him to the doctor.' Minutes later

Sugiati came running to find her, clearly distressed. 'Come quickly, Sus Anne. It's Danang. He's dead.'

Anne asked her visitors for help to transport him at once to the hospital, but all attempts to revive him failed. She was devastated by the suddenness of events and with Christmas very near the loss of a child was so poignant. At the request of his parents Anne made arrangements for the little boy to be buried. Pak Timan and Pak Mesdi made a little coffin and the children made a cross. The coffin was lined with nappies and the tiny body placed tenderly in it. Bambang was one of the two members of the Yayasan who came regularly to Beth Shan and he conducted a little service for the children and staff.

That same afternoon the Toyota pick-up was delivered and it was used to carry the coffin through the pouring rain to the cemetery.

They drove along the rough mud-caked track used by the Beth Shan family every Sunday on their way to church and although Anne was afraid they would land in the ditch they arrived without mishap with their precious cargo and Danang was laid to rest.

Using their pocket money the children had collected enough to purchase a Bible, and inside the front cover Anang drew a picture of

Jesus, the Good Shepherd, carrying Danang in His arms.

In accordance with Javanese custom a memorial service was held a week later at Danang's home and people came from far and near. At the parents' request the service was conducted by Pastor Ayub, a member of the Yayasan. Some of the older children went with Anne and during the service she presented to the parents the Bible the children had bought as a memorial gift from Beth Shan.

The parents were only nominally Muslim and when the service was over they offered to open their home as a meeting place for a weekly Sunday School. Within a month both parents were soundly converted and established a fellowship in their home. Some three years later Anne had the great privilege of attending the opening of the church that the believers had built themselves.

8

1983 – 1984

*A much needed furlough. The Kopeng
project. A cot death.*

Early in 1983 a family of four children arrived
from West Java; a tragic little group ranging
in age from five to fourteen years. Daniel
Kurniawan, Eva, Lukas and Petrus. When their
mother discovered that her husband was
planning to take a second wife she had doused
herself with kerosene, and in front of the
children set fire to herself. Very shortly
afterwards the father was knocked down by a
truck and killed.

The children had a grandmother but she was
too elderly to care for such a large family, and
they were brought to Beth Shan by their local
pastor and his wife. Anne knew it would be a
long time before they experienced any measure
of emotional healing.

Education was still considered a privilege
in Indonesia and was very expensive and Anne
was greatly relieved in getting all four children

into school. With limited places available things might not have worked out so smoothly.

Audrey Corser returned to Beth Shan at the end of May to a rapturous welcome from the children and Anne decided to take a brief trip home. Pak Mesdi had now passed his driving test and with the pick-up converted into a station wagon he proudly took on the role of family chauffeur!

Kuntum, who had joined the family in 1981, came from a strong Muslim background and was proving difficult to control. His father had recently remarried and his new wife was just eighteen years old. Kuntum was fifteen himself and deeply resented his stepmother. Although unwilling at first his father agreed to let his son return home and he left with the prayers of all at Beth Shan following him. His Muslim beliefs had remained strong and he refused the Bible offered to him when he left but he did accept a copy of Nicky Cruz' *Run, Baby, Run*.

Kunyil was found roaming the streets by a university teacher and in spite of the fact that she was dirty and neglected the teacher could see how undernourished she was and took her home to give her a meal. She discovered that the girl was homeless and had no parents and efforts to trace any relatives led nowhere.

She was an epileptic with a very low I.Q.

and in May, when the Welfare Department had provided the necessary papers, she was brought to Beth Shan.

Her arm and leg had been broken in a motorbike accident and with no treatment given at the time her bones had knit together, causing deformities. It would require surgery and lengthy hospitalization to improve her physical condition.

Yunaten arrived at Beth Shan at the tender age of just four days and was soon adopted into the family of a Christian pastor whose home was in East Java. It was a joy to know that the child would be nurtured in a loving Christian environment.

Towards the end of May the village chief arrived at Beth Shan bringing with him a baby girl. She was just twelve hours old and had been rescued by neighbours when they heard that she was going to be thrown into the river. The family named her Ribkah.

In the meantime Anne was enjoying a warm and sunny English summer and was delighted to be home and to have the opportunity to share time and news with family and friends.

She attended a conference in Switzerland, at the place where so many years before she had taken parties of deprived children, and it was a special joy to stay in the home of Jean

André whose prayerful support had been such an encouragement to her.

Despite his advanced years he was still very active for God and was currently running camps for Polish children. What a host of memories flooded back as she talked and shared with him. It was good to have the opportunity to renew old friendships and to form new ones as she shared the joys and the needs of the Beth Shan family.

She was naturally missing them all but regular news from Audrey, together with letters and drawings from the children, kept her in touch and warmed her heart.

She heard that Kunyil had undergone surgery and was now receiving post-operative care at home. In hospital she had refused to co-operate, bewildered no doubt by the sudden and alarming changes in her life. Initial feeding problems with Ribkah were now resolved and she was beginning to put on weight.

Beth Shan was currently negotiating for the purchase of 8,000 square metres of land in the mountains of Central Java, and it was a great thrill for Anne to be able to share news of this project with her prayer supporters at home. Her vision was to build an Outreach and Retreat Centre to accommodate those in need of refreshment and renewal. Plans were already being drawn up and subject to a clear 'go ahead' from God the work was expected to begin early in 1984.

Special prayers were sought that all the government deadlines would be met by mid-September without any problems or hitches.

Eight-year-old Elisa sent Anne more family news. 'Guess what, Mami,' she wrote. 'Kunyil is getting better and she helps Menik put the washing on the lines and she says her prayers before she eats. Mami, she even puts her hands together!' A letter from Audrey confirmed that Kunyil was indeed making good progress.

There had been another new arrival during Anne's absence, a five-month-old boy named Saprianto, and Anne longed to be back at Beth Shan to hold the newest member of her family in her arms.

Before she left England she received the great news that God had miraculously provided for the purchase of land at Kopeng where the Conference Centre would be built. On November 14th, 1983, with anticipation in her heart, she was on her way.

Audrey and several of the children were at Solo Airport to meet her and the warmth of their welcome left Anne in no doubt about their delight at having her back.

She noticed thoughtful, sidelong glances

from some of the younger children, uncertain about why she had been away so long and wondering whether or not she was now home to stay. It was all very confusing!

Audrey appeared to have stood up well to the endless demands made upon her during Anne's furlough, in spite of adjustments to a vastly different culture, climate and diet. Anne soon became aware, however, that life at Beth Shan during her absence had not been without its difficulties.

Anang, now sixteen years old, was still battling with deep emotional trauma from his past. He wanted to be circumcised like his Muslim friends but at the same time he wanted to be a follower of Jesus Christ. Audrey had found him difficult to cope with and Anne could see more problems looming ahead.

With Christmas not far away she was soon involved in the busyness of preparations and with the rough and tumble of everyday life in a very large family. A local factory gave a sackful of cloth pieces as a Christmas gift and every available pair of hands was busily sewing the pieces together to make sheets for the new Conference Centre at Kopeng.

Three visitors arrived from New Zealand and Audrey and Anne had the joy of sharing with them in a traditional English breakfast on

Christmas morning. It was inevitable, though, that at unexpected moments their thoughts would turn to Christmas celebrations taking place hundreds of miles away at home.

On Christmas Eve a tropical storm caused serious flooding as the river in the village overflowed its banks and supplies of water and electricity failed. A further storm on Christmas Day resulted in the now restored electricity being cut off again, and when the hand pump broke down two drums of water had to be brought in for household purposes. Christmas by candlelight, though not from choice, was nonetheless a joyous occasion, and young voices sang 'Happy Birthday' to Jesus with sincerity and great gusto.

Kunyil was missing! After much frantic searching she was discovered in a ditch lying face down in three inches of water. She was not at all happy at being disturbed and objected strongly to having a bath and being put in a clean bed.

Kaka the cockatoo had been accidentally sprayed with a mosquito spray instead of water and in spite of every effort to revive him he died. It was Anne's first experience of giving the kiss of life to a cockatoo! Life at Beth Shan was certainly never dull!

One of the village children attending the kindergarten school suffered a hard blow from a swing and remained unconscious for several days. In spite of the negative opinion of the doctor the child regained consciousness and made a gradual but complete recovery. Hospitalization had been essential and now the family was left with high medical fees which they were unable to meet.

They lived just across the road from Beth Shan and once again, through what at first appeared to be a disaster, God opened a door. Anne offered them a loan to help pay their debt and they responded by opening both their hearts and their home to the gospel. Later in the year, instead of having special Christmas food, the children voted to thank God for Jesus by giving all that they had to this needy family.

The legal details for the purchase of the land at Kopeng were at last completed and Anne was thrilled. The Yayasan gave her vision their full backing and although the purchase of the land was her responsibility they offered to help with the buying of materials and the oversight of the building programme.

Anne firmly believed that her vision was of God but was equally certain that she was not meant to be involved in the running of the Conference Centre. There would need to be a

Christian couple in charge who had a vision for spiritual growth among the young people of Indonesia.

Anne's visa was due for renewal in March and when she was granted just a temporary one expiring on June 18th she knew that it was time to go ahead and apply for Indonesian citizenship. It was a big step prompted by her concern for the continued right to care for her family. How could she possibly abandon the children whom God had so clearly placed in her care?

Early in March Pak Surgiato joined the staff as driver of the fourteen seater pick-up and was launched into his new post with a four-hour drive to Wonsobo to collect Yanto and Lidia from school for the holidays. It proved to be a tough 'breaking in' experience! On the way back they ran into a tropical storm with driving rain and high winds uprooting trees and causing extensive damage to houses and crops. Visibility was almost nil. Due to broken bridges and blocked roads Surgiato was redirected three times and even then disaster was narrowly avoided. As they drove along the road a huge tree was uprooted and started to fall across their path. They managed to escape, only to see another large tree crashing down towards their vehicle and landing just a matter of inches away from them. All three were very badly shaken when eventually they arrived safely back at Beth Shan. What protection God had afforded – and what an introduction for Pak Surgiato to his new job!

Saprianto, now a year old, was adopted by a missionary family in Salawesi, one of Indonesia's largest islands. Newly introduced laws now stated that non-nationals could no longer adopt unless they had been resident in the country for at least three years.

Yohan had joined the family in 1981 when he was just five months old and now he was going home. His mother had undergone cancer surgery which proved successful and with her health renewed she was longing to take her child home.

She was a lovely Christian girl for whom the pain of parting with Yohan had only been bearable because she knew that at Beth Shan he would be loved and nurtured in the ways of the Lord.

Anang, in spite of all his problems, decided to start High School in July and Anne felt encouraged. He was very gifted in art and in playing the guitar and she was sure that he had a genuine desire to continue to live as a Christian. He would, however, need much prayer and support.

It was July 17th, 1984 and Anne was returning from a Church Congress in Salawesi. As the pedicab stopped outside Beth Shan she knew instinctively that all was not well. Children and staff rushed out to welcome her, some in tears and all talking at once. 'Mami, Sugiati's gone to hospital'. 'Mami, Sugiati's dead'. Fear gripped Anne's heart as she tried to find out what was wrong and as she began to grasp the facts her concern deepened.

The day had begun just like any other with all the normal routine jobs completed by lunchtime.

When siesta time was over Sugiati had gone to collect six-month-old Emiliana from her cot, having prepared her bath and her feeding bottle. As she picked the baby up she discovered to her horror that the child was dead. The shock was so great that Sugiati had collapsed and did not regain consciousness for six hours. For the rest of the family panic and hysteria took over and Anne's return was clearly God's timing.

A death certificate was issued by the doctor together with a donation of £50 to cover burial costs. A small coffin was bought and lined with white cotton and the children found comfort in their grief as they made garlands with frangipanni flowers.

The following morning, after a short service,

they began the three-mile journey to the cemetery. Anang and Kurniawan carried the coffin to the grave-side, and as the little body was laid to rest the children sang together 'Safe in the arms of Jesus'. Yesterday she had been a normal, happy baby; now she was dead; and the family was devastated.

Desianti, Elisa's sister, had to be led away from the grave-side. She was eight years old and deeply distressed. 'I can't leave her there all by herself, Mami,' she sobbed, 'She will get so cold'. Painful memories of lost loved ones were stirred and Anne spent the remainder of the day giving comfort and support to many of her children.

Quite a number had been bereaved of both parents and her heart ached as she tried to answer their questions. 'Lap ministry' was very important but it was also very time consuming.

This latest crisis caused further feelings of panic to surface as Anne waited for news of her citizenship papers and for a year's extension on her visa. What would become of her children if she was forced to leave the country? Pontas Pardede, with the advantages of his legal standing, went to Jakarta and personally placed Anne's official request for citizenship with the two departments involved.

Johannes unexpectedly left Beth Shan

following the remarriage of his mother, with his new stepfather insisting that the child was now his responsibility. Anne watched him go with mixed feelings, aware that his constant tantrums and outbursts had placed a great strain on all the staff, but all the same, it would feel strange without him.

Kristianto also went home, having lived at Beth Shan since 1981. His father had suffered a complete mental breakdown following his wife's desertion, but now he was fully recovered and had recently become a Christian. Such bright gleams of information came as encouragement in the midst of many needs and difficulties.

There was another problem that could no longer be ignored. Beth Shan was once again bursting at the seams! A family of five children was due to arrive at any time and the number of children would then reach forty-five!

Once again Anne met with the Yayasan for urgent consultations. They would need to build as soon as possible – not out, but up! A second storey would have to be added to Beth Shan.

It would be a major project involving the removal of the roof from the front section of the house to add sufficient accommodation for Anne and sleeping quarters for the girls and the babies. With the Kopeng project also in the pipeline she experienced serious misgivings in her heart, but clearly something had to be done.

She was informed that her visa had been extended to March 1985 and by the end of November her citizenship papers were all placed in Jakarta. Now she must wait for the consent of the Minister of Religion before the final processing could go ahead. What a relief it would be when this final hurdle was overcome.

Joko was four years old when he joined the family in 1979. Weakened by malnutrition and tuberculosis his fight back to health was long and difficult, and as a result of deep trauma in his early years he was very withdrawn.

Anne had twice been asked to remove him from school where he had been assessed as having no learning ability. Extra help and attention at home had yielded no obvious results – until one day he seemed suddenly to come to life. By the end of 1984 he had made remarkable progress and to the amazement of his teachers gained a result of 100% in three different tests. There were great celebrations at Beth Shan!

One day in November Anang disappeared and all efforts to trace him failed. Anne was very distressed, not only because of the deep emotional scars he carried but also because she was aware of his great potential. She vowed never to stop searching and praying until he was safely home again.

The plans for a second storey at Beth Shan, together with the plans for Kopeng, were submitted to the authorities for their approval, but with the arrival of the rainy season it would be some time before work could commence.

Towards the end of November the family received three-week-old Amelyia Oktriana with mixed emotions. As a result of the recent cot death of Emiliana the staff were apprehensive about handling her and unwilling to be responsible for her care. Three weeks earlier a local person had sent a parcel to Beth Shan containing tinned milk and baby food. It had seemed so cruel at the time but now Anne saw yet again the outworking of God's purposes.

At Christmas the family gathered to celebrate and to give thanks for the Babe of Bethlehem. It was a poignant occasion.

9

1985 – 1988

A second storey. Heart surgery.
Kopeng foundations laid.

1985 dawned with still no definite news of the long awaited family of five children. It emerged that as a result of death threats they had been forced to flee from their home in West Java and were taken into hiding at a secret location in Solo. With their father still alive the Yayasan refused to accept them without a covering letter from the courts, yet in spite of the circumstances the local school agreed to take them. Staff from Beth Shan collected them from their secret location each morning and escorted them to school, also providing them with two meals every day. When school was over they were returned safely to their Solo hideout for the night. The mother was a sick woman, and with four of the children suffering from tuberculosis it was hoped that they could be moved into Beth Shan by the end of January.

It was agreed that the building project at Beth Shan should begin once the rains stopped.

As she visualised the busy months ahead Anne was concerned that in the midst of so much activity and bustle the children would not be deprived of the love and attention they so badly needed.

Dani Kristianto arrived home from school one day with severe breathing difficulties and was immediately hospitalised. He was diagnosed as having mitral stenosis with lung complications and within ten days he was admitted to hospital in Jakarta to undergo major heart surgery.

A young Christian couple living in Jakarta were due to travel to the U.K. for a holiday and offered Anne the use of their home while they were away. How wonderfully God always provided for her needs! In the meantime many prayers were being offered for Dani's healing.

A few months before Dani's illness, while Anne was having her hair cut, her hairdresser had thrust seven grams of gold into her hand, telling her, to her great surprise, that she wanted Anne to receive it as a gift. That gold, together with the sale of some gold ear-rings, secured the necessary deposit for Dani's surgery. God's clear provision was almost overwhelming! There is no National Health Service in Indonesia and Anne was aware that the medical costs involved for the operation and subsequent medical care would be great. She would also be required to cover all his nursing care while he remained in hospital and decided that she would stay with him during the first two critical post-operative weeks with other Beth Shan staff sharing the burden as he began to recover.

Meanwhile the building of a second storey for Beth Shan was going ahead with school holidays adding to the general chaos and confusion.

Somehow fifty children were fitted into three rooms with some of the girls sleeping two in a bed and others on the floor. The boys moved into the dining room, the toddlers and babies were together in the one remaining room, while Anne herself took up residence in the laundry! The heat was almost unbearable!

The boys rose to the occasion in great style, clearing up the debris when the workmen left at three o'clock each afternoon, and leaving everything ready for them to start again the following day.

The five children in hiding in Solo were now able safely to move into Beth Shan and proved to be quite delinquent, causing havoc to the point where maintaining discipline became almost impossible.

Dani's mother was on her way to visit him after his operation when she suddenly collapsed and died. Her baby daughter, born out of wedlock, was just nine months old. The grandmother did what she could but with no income and a baby to feed she soon got into debt. Threats were made to steal and sell the baby if she did not pay her debtors and early one morning she arrived at Beth Shan in great panic and distress. She vowed that however fearful she was she would never allow the child to become the property of people who did not love her.

There was little that Anne could do without the necessary papers but when she contacted the Social Welfare Department they agreed that the child should be admitted while they waited for the mother's death certificate. Her name was Natalia and with medical care and a proper diet she quickly responded and began to gain weight.

By now the roof of Beth Shan had been removed and there seemed to be bamboo scaffolding everywhere. August 17th was Indonesia's Independence Day and this gave the family a break and the opportunity to be together and to celebrate eleven birthdays – some a bit late and others a bit early! It was a happy and relaxed day with party fare, a birthday cake and gifts – to the great delight of the children.

By mid-August Dani was making excellent

progress. His final checkup was due in September and he eagerly anticipated the day, longing to be able once more to participate in school sports.

A special Thanksgiving Day was arranged for November 25th, and with the building work now completed and Dani able once more to live a normal life, there was much to celebrate. To add to the general excitement each child received a present.

A special visitor for the occasion was George Rabey, General Secretary of Unevangelised Fields Mission (U.F.M.) to which Anne was affiliated. It was a rather unusual Thanksgiving Day but nonetheless a very joyful occasion.

A month later, very early on Christmas morning, the staff assembled together and went from room to room singing carols to the children as they lay in bed and giving each one a small wrapped gift. A further gift of turkey cooked in coconut milk provided the Christmas meal, sufficient to feed seventy hungry people!

In the evening the family held a 'Get Together' with the children presenting gifts to Anne and all the members of the staff.

They had bought them with their own money and arranged them in beautifully decorated boxes, together with sweets and home-made coconut cakes. Half an hour before the party was due to start there was a loud knock at the door – a visitor had arrived to deliver a two-foot-square Christmas cake! What a faithful God who even provides 'extras' for a special occasion!

When finally the year drew to its close Anne looked back with emotions that were a mixture of thankfulness and relief, and as she considered all that had been achieved she was aware that it was only God who could make those achievements of lasting worth.

'Dig the ditches!' The short, clear message was given to Anne while she was praying about the Kopeng project early in 1986.

In addition to the new laws about Christian meetings there was also another problem to be resolved. Water was not laid on at the building site and this was essential before any building work could begin.

Initial permission had been given to build a villa for the Beth Shan family and seeing this as a good starting point Anne and the Yayasan were encouraged. Coffee, orange and clove trees were planted on the land to provide an income that would help towards further education costs for the children, but the coffee trees failed to produce and died. There was much prayer for the right contacts in the building trade, for honest and reliable workmen, and for fair prices as the necessary materials were bargained for.

In the meantime Audrey Corser made another welcome return to Beth Shan and Anne took the opportunity to return to England for a two-month furlough.

With growing certainty about her application to become an Indonesian citizen and with her involvement in the new village church which had been built close to the kindergarten school, Anne recognised that this was the right time for her to resign her membership at West Kilburn Baptist Church.

Although in many ways it was a painful decision she knew that her links with the fellowship there would remain.

During her time in England she had looked more and more upon Leicester as her base, and because it had remained her mother's home it was also a place where she could begin to get her roots down. Her mother worked tirelessly to gain spiritual and practical support for the work at Beth Shan and this, too, played an important part in giving Anne a sense of 'belonging'.

While Anne was in England the staff at Beth

Shan had a surprise visit from Anang, bringing a friend with him. He now had a job and looked well and the staff welcomed him warmly, eager to hear all his news. Dani, however, refused to speak to him. Anang had been his closest friend at Beth Shan and as he struggled with his own deep emotional problems Anang became just one more person who had failed him and let him down.

Audrey stayed at Beth Shan until the end of August and when she returned to England Anne missed her keenly. It meant so much to be able to converse in her own language and to share and pray together. Often they had wept and often laughed, and this was especially precious in a culture that was so different from her own. It pleased her that Audrey had clearly established her own place in the hearts of the Beth Shan family.

The children had recently been given several musical instruments and they decided to form an orchestra. One of the local church members offered to teach them how to play well and with their natural sense of rhythm the results were quite remarkable.

The little ones were given pea-shakers so that no-one was excluded from the fun and Beth Shan became a place of music, even if there were occasions when calling it 'a joyful noise unto the Lord' was perhaps a somewhat generous compliment!

The foundation stones for the house at Kopeng were laid in September 1986. A carpenter in Solo had already been busy making windows and doors in readiness for the start of the building work and the pick-up was used to transport them to the site. With a variety of timbers being used it was necessary to get a special permit from the Forestry Commission to move wood from one district to another, mainly to prevent stealing from the teak forests.

As the building progressed Pak Timan and Pak Mesdi spent a lot of time at Kopeng overseeing the project with two good men employed to do the actual building work. Although the water supply had now been paid for there was still delay in laying the pipes and this became a matter of some concern as a water supply was essential for the work to go ahead.

Mavis Pardede, the wife of Pontas, was also Anne's colleague in the work at Beth Shan, and towards the end of the year both she and Anne went down with typhoid, probably as a result of drinking unboiled water. It proved a most debilitating illness and it was some time before they were fully recovered.

During the holidays Anne arranged a Christmas card competition, calling in outside people to act as judges. Many of the children had natural artistic talents and the results of their efforts were most impressive.

From this developed a project enabling the children to earn money as they produced packs of hand-painted Christmas cards to be sold in East and West Java. With the proceeds of their work the children began to breed chicken and it became a most successful project.

With Anne's continued links with the Jean André homes in Switzerland Beth Shan decided to 'adopt' and pray for six Polish children, and in spite of the thousands of miles that separated them the children were thrilled to be involved. It was now two years since parties of Polish children had begun to visit Switzerland and there had been much blessing and answered prayer. The enthusiasm of her children delighted Anne, knowing that this would help to enlarge their vision of God's work in other parts of the world.

In Solo a group of missionaries began to meet together once a month to pray for a move of the Holy Spirit throughout Indonesia.

On Christmas Eve an operetta was shown on television clearly proclaiming the Word of God and in the shops of Solo Christian tapes were played.

On December 30th Anne went with the

older children to a sports stadium in Solo where 3,000 people were gathered for a Christmas celebration of praise. Anne whispered to Paulus who was sitting beside her 'Isn't this amazing! There are so many people here and we know hardly any of them yet God is watching over each one in a special way.' It was a wonderful note on which to end a busy and exciting year.

Early in the New Year Anne was delighted to receive a letter from Bill and Tricia McIlroy asking if they might visit her in June and spend a month at Beth Shan. Bill was the minister of West Kilburn Baptist Church where Anne had until recently been a member. He had attended the official opening of Beth Shan in 1978 bringing with him the letter from Anne's uncle informing her of her father's sudden death. How long ago it all seemed now – and what a difference he would see when he arrived, both in the building and in the size of the family!

A visit to the U.S.A. in April was also on Anne's agenda, linking up with her mother and brother to share in a family reunion. It looked like being another exciting year!

New children continued to arrive and it was good to watch them slowly settle in and find their niche in the Beth Shan family. It was good, too, to see a measure of progress in children who had previously arrived with deep needs of both physical and emotional healing for their damaged lives. Those coming into their teenage years struggled with their own particular battles and heartaches, and Anne was thankful for the support of a dedicated and competent staff.

Limin had just completed a course at Pontas' Bible School and was back at Beth Shan seeking God's will for the next step in her life. Should she become a teacher, or maybe a nurse? She was content to wait until God clearly showed her the way forward.

Once again tropical storms caused havoc, with serious flooding and extensive damage to buildings. Anne slipped on a wet floor and her arm was in a plaster cast for several weeks. The pain and restriction in practical things was something she found frustrating and hard to bear, but bear it she must!

Dani continued to grow stronger with encouraging reports following his latest checkup but his attitude and behaviour remained very difficult, creating endless problems for the staff and repercussions on the children. One of the teenage girls was proving such a bad influence on the other children that Anne was forced to make a difficult decision. A telegram was sent to her mother asking her to collect her daughter and take her home, and it was with a heavy

left: The house at Baron (pg 40)
top right: Suriadi, 4 yrs (pg 49/50)
bottom right: Adi, 4 yrs Beth
Shans first child (pg 47/48)

The 'new' Beth Shan, early 1978 (pg 72)

top left: Audrey Corser
'A birthday party', 1987
(pg 139)

bottom left: Anne Dakin with
some of the children 1989

right: Anne Dakin, Taking the
Oath of Allegiance 1989
(pg 159)

top left: Kitty Hay with Endang outside Beth Shan 1990 (pg 81/82)
top right: Sheila Few nursing Jadid who died Feb 2000 (pg 169, 222)
bottom: Anne with Lusi, 13 yrs and Munarsih, 15 yrs, 1990 (pg 54, 179)

top: Pastor Ayub Lande (pastor of Cemani Church and member of the Yayasan) and his wife Diana, July 1990 (pg 162, 215)
bottom: Pastor Ayub greets Anne outside Cemani Church

Beth Shan with 2nd storey completed 1995 (pg 191)

Meleina, 10 yrs, 1998 (pg 150)

Untung, 9 yrs, 1998 (pg 160)

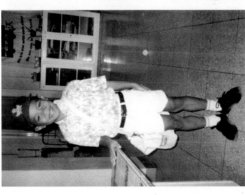

Robi, 8 yrs, 1998 (pg164)

At the end of the story.
A special cake to celebrate
25yrs and a new
millennium.

heart that Anne bade her farewell.

She felt it would be good to establish a 'family evening' when all the children could be present to talk and share together as a family, but with the inevitable and unpredictable crises never far away it was an arrangement that was not easy to maintain.

She had a wonderful time in America and was especially thrilled to meet up with relatives she had not seen for many years. Sugiati had again been left in charge at Beth Shan and with total confidence in her ability to cope Anne was able to relax and enjoy herself.

On her way back to Java she had an unexpected stopover day in London and the flowers and shrubs in gardens and parks were refreshment to her soul.

It was Sunday and although she had to remain within reasonable distance of the airport she was able to meet up with friends and attend a church service with them, participating in the singing, listening to the Bible readings and an excellent sermon – all in her mother tongue! It was indeed a feast of good things.

The excited group of children waiting to greet her at Solo Airport soon dealt with any lingering feelings of homesickness. During her absence Prihartini had joined the family, having been brought to Sugiati by a worker from the Social Welfare Department. She had been abandoned at birth and was picked up from the streets by the police at just seven days old. She was suffering from venereal disease and had badly infected eyes, and for the first five months she was nursed in isolation with eye drops administered every twenty minutes night and day.

Kurniawan, although still nervous and shy, was developing into a fine young man but had not yet made a definite commitment of his life to Jesus Christ. He was eighteen and in the middle of his final exams, anxious to do well and to secure for himself a place at university. The alternative would be to leave home and find work in Jakarta, a prospect that did not appeal to him at all.

The first part of the building project at Kopeng was nearing completion and it was planned that some of the older children should stay there during May to plant out the land and the garden and complete the internal painting work.

Anne hoped that Bill and Tricia McIlroy would be the first visitors to occupy the house when they arrived in June.

Yanto was keen to leave the special school for the deaf so many miles away and to register in an ordinary High School in Solo. He was now able to lip read extremely well and had developed into a fine and sensitive teenager.

In July the family was joined by members of the Yayasan and their wives to celebrate another Thanksgiving Day. It was now an incredible twelve years since the first such occasion at the little house in Baron and it was another opportunity to look back and give thanks to a faithful and protecting God.

There was great rejoicing when Dani Kristianto came top in his school exams, gaining for himself a prize of six months free education.

Kurniawan graduated from sixth form and a university place was now a definite possibility. He had also taken a stand for the Lord and testified to his newly found faith as he went through the waters of baptism. It was a moving occasion.

Yanto succeeded in gaining a place in secondary school bringing to an end the long periods of time spent away at boarding school.

Anne confessed to some anxiety when he told her that he intended to cycle the two miles to school each day – it would not be easy for a deaf boy on roads that were always very busy and where the Highway Code was unheard of.

The family of five children from West Java who had caused such disruption had now been returned to their father, and Paulus, who had been very much the ringleader when they

147

arrived, opted to remain at Beth Shan. God had clearly been working in his heart.

With problems about the water system at Kopeng still unresolved it was decided that another water pump would have to be installed and a new well sunk. After a long period of drought the rains had arrived, but rejoicing was short-lived, for they came with such force that many homes were destroyed or washed away. It was a difficult time for Menik who had now been on the staff for seven years and lived with her parents not far from Beth Shan. Her parents were both unwell, particularly her father who was now very elderly, which meant that Menik was the only breadwinner. Their home was built close to the river's edge and was flooded when the river finally burst its banks. Anne had a special concern for Menik who was from a mixed-race background and could not read or write.

Daud recovered slowly from a severe bout of flu, repeatedly asking for 'Daddy'. It had been confirmed that he would not be eligible for adoption and he became very weepy and possessive of Anne, creating a difficult situation for her with so many other children also needing individual attention.

The Toyota pick-up was now six years old and continued to give invaluable service. Anne decided to take a group of children on a day's outing to the foothills of Mount Merapi, one of Indonesia's most active volcanoes. The weather did not look too promising as they set out, and as the now well-worn Toyota chugged its way up and around the narrow hairpin bends a foggy mist started to descend.

The temperature dropped and gale force winds battered the vehicle, leaving the group equally battered and worn as they started the return trip home. 'Thank God,' thought Anne, 'that the Holy Spirit comes into our lives as a gentle breeze and not a gale-force wind.'

Anne was delighted when she received news that her application for Indonesian citizenship had been approved, and she awaited the summons to be sworn in with deep and mixed emotions. A few days earlier she had been totally overwhelmed when an anonymous donor from Jakarta presented Beth Shan with a second vehicle, brand new and specially designed to accommodate the needs of such a large family. There seemed to be no words to express to God the awe and thankfulness that filled her heart.

The older children continued to give a lot of help and support, with some busily digging the foundations for a new garage, some stripping down the bathroom walls ready for repainting and others putting a fresh coat of paint on the dining room chairs.

Sugiati's life was full and busy. She would spend the mornings working at Beth Shan, returning home at two o'clock to spend a couple of hours cooking for her family and preparing savoury meatball soup to sell at the roadside. Somehow she always managed to roll out of bed in time to be on duty at Beth Shan by five o'clock each morning, no doubt spurred on by the knowledge that this was the only way to make it possible to put their two sons through school.

Meilina, tiny and very beautiful, was born on May 27th, 1988. Her mother was unmarried and had stayed close to Beth Shan during the final months of her pregnancy. She was a good baby, but night feeds were an exhausting business at the end of a busy day.

Dani was now experiencing severe bouts of depression and as a result of getting into bad company at school he repeatedly threatened to run away. In the end, knowing that she must deal with the situation, Anne told him that in view of his repeated threats she had decided to give him permission to leave Beth Shan. Her words took Dani completely by surprise and proved to be the right approach. He confessed that he did not really want to leave Beth Shan and promised that he would make a real effort to get his life sorted out if he was allowed to stay.

In mid-July Audrey Corser, beloved 'tante Emi' to all the children, again came to visit the family, and Anne decided to take a furlough in England, and when she returned in November she brought her mother back with her.

Retti was a qualified secretary and she now joined the staff and quickly established an efficient office routine. She had been trained by the Yayasan and her expertise meant that Anne could relinquish her administrative responsibilities and did so with great relief! Again there was a need for more helpers and it was decided that with so many of the children now in their teens very young staff would no longer be considered.

To accommodate an unexpected gift of some statues the children built a fish pond near the front entrance where they could stand proudly among the fish and the water lilies.

Towards the end of the year Li Sen, who had been at Beth Shan since 1976, and Ester, half-brother of Dani, both became Christians. Li Sen was a natural musician and loved to play the drums, and it was thrilling to see two more young lives so wonderfully transformed.

In November, Ibu Lasut joined the staff and was given the responsibility of looking after Sutrisno and Jadid who both suffered from severe cerebral palsy. Anne was touched by her obvious love and patience as she cared for the two tragic little boys, and in her heart gave thanks again for such a good and loyal team of workers.

The house at Kopeng could now comfortably accommodate forty people and Anne took the children there whenever she could.

The beauty of the mountains and the surrounding countryside was quite breathtaking, and to gather around a wood fire in the evenings when it became cold was a special thrill and gave a great feeling of closeness.

Wahyu, a little boy of seven, came from the mountains of Kopeng to join the family. He had been deserted by his father when he was just three weeks old, and because his mother was blind she was not able to look after him. He had been living with his grandmother whose home was about six miles from Kopeng, but now she was too old to cope and too poor to send him to school.

Once his crying and distress were spent he began to respond to love, and as soon as he was more settled he eagerly began to learn to read and write. He had never heard of Christmas and when the festive season arrived with all its celebrations he was filled with wonder and delight.

At nine o'clock on New Year's Eve Anne

and the older children left Beth Shan, wending their way through the village, over the bridge and past the fields of sugar cane, to the church, where a number of folk from the village were already gathered.

Together they thanked God for all the blessings of the past year and prayed for His guidance and provision for the year that lay ahead. So much had happened during 1988. What would 1989 hold? Anne knew her own weaknesses and inadequacies only too well, especially the all-too-frequent moments of impatience and irritation that so easily came to the surface.

All the same her heart rejoiced in the God who loved and understood her and who knew far better than she ever could the needs of each child committed to her care.

Her eyes wandered along the row of teenagers beside her, aware of the traumas that had so deeply scarred their lives. Her gaze rested on Elisa, Dani, Cap Sen, Yanto and Kurniawan, and in the silence of her heart she whispered her New Year prayer.

'I said any time, anywhere, Lord, without any idea of the implications, but now I truly understand. I stand here tonight much wiser, more mature and somewhat battered, but I still mean every word.'

10

1989 – 1990

An Indonesian citizen. Some heart searching. Camping.

It was mid-January and the house at Kopeng was filled with the sounds of laughter and excited chatter. With primary school exams finished Anne had arrived with a large group of children for a four-day break.

It was lunchtime, and with the family gathered around the meal table she read aloud from the Book of Psalms. Joko had chosen the reading and Anne was moved as she listened to the reasons he gave for his choice. His childhood years had been painful and traumatic and at fifteen he remained silent and withdrawn. While very young he had lost the sight of an eye and the learning difficulties with which he still struggled were just one outcome of malnutrition and tuberculosis in his early years. 'There is no hope for this child', the education authorities had told Anne, but now to the amazement of both his teachers and the staff at Beth Shan his grades were gradually improving.

The noise of the generator droning in the background was lost as praises to God from lusty young throats echoed around the mountains of Kopeng.

Quietly Joko joined in as the children sang 'Thank you, O my Father, for giving us Your Son and leaving Your Spirit till the work on earth is done'. In her heart Anne thanked God for all that He had done, and would yet do, in the life of Joko.

With a few teething troubles still to be resolved it had been decided not to build or expand further at Kopeng for the time being, but already the house had proved a blessing to the various groups who had stayed there.

A local couple had recently been appointed to act as caretakers and to receive visitors on behalf of Beth Shan and Anne hoped to use the house herself from time to time as a place of retreat, affording brief respite from the constant demands of her ever-growing family.

Doctors diagnosed brain damage and encephalitis when Prahyude arrived at Beth Shan and a neurologist in Yogyakarta was appointed to monitor his progress. There was great rejoicing when a report stated that he was responding well to treatment and that brain damage was minimal. His ability to speak had been affected but now he was beginning to talk, and running to meet Anne one day as she returned from a shopping trip he shouted 'Ami. Ami'. Anne was confident that before long he would be saying 'Mami. Mami'.

With their sights now firmly set on university Lukas and Cap Sen were studying hard and were always keen to do any jobs that would earn money to help pay the expensive university fees. They were both teaching in Sunday School and the younger boys idolised them.

Many of the older children were also studying hard to secure a place at senior High School although Anne realised that they would not all be successful. Whatever the outcome it was good to encourage the discipline and effort that serious study demanded.

Sabdinator, known affectionately as Sab, had also set his sights on university and had definite ability, but his sense of humour and general high spirits often landed him in trouble. Beth Shan staff would shrug their shoulders in despair at his antics but they knew that at heart he was a good boy.

Eight-year-old Setyo had been deserted by his mother while still a toddler and struggled daily with the pain and trauma of knowing that he had been rejected. He tended to isolate himself from the other children and was inattentive at school, making little progress. Realising his need for individual attention Anne set aside time to spend with him to help him learn to relate, and slowly her efforts bore fruit as he began to establish his own identity. When he was particularly naughty and difficult to control Anne was tempted to leave him to his own devices; it was so much easier to concentrate on less complicated children, but she knew that this was not God's way.

At seven months Nataniel was slow to develop and made no effort to sit up, while Meilina, now eight months old, was hardly ever still. Soon she would be taking her first faltering steps and had established herself as a great favourite with staff and children alike.

Staff changes were more frequent than Anne would have wished and the need for a long-term helper was now a matter of some urgency. Further changes in Indonesian law continued to give cause for concern with all missionaries now limited to a ten-year stay in the country. They were also required to have a theological degree and to be attached to a Bible School. These latest changes convinced Anne that she would not really be secure until she had become an Indonesian citizen.

Aware of the enormity of this step and

knowing that a number of her friends thought that she was making a mistake, Anne arranged to talk the matter through with a friend. He was a godly Christian man and she knew that he would give her wise counsel.

He had no idea what was on her heart when they met but before she began to explain he told her that he believed God had given him a word to pass on to her. It was a verse from the Book of Revelation, 'They overcame by the blood of the Lamb and by the word of their testimony and they loved not their lives unto death'. His prayer for her before they parted was 'Whatever the future holds for Anne, dear Lord, be it life or death, may she know Your grip upon her life'. Early in 1989 Anne took the Oath of Allegiance and was given a piece of paper bearing the signature of President Suharto and stating that she now belonged to the Indonesian people.

She had her papers! Yes, it was a big step but what a relief to know that she could continue to be a mother to her children with no more fear of visas not being renewed. Now she really belonged!

At a small family celebration Cap Sen prayed that she would be a 'good Indonesian citizen', and a couple of days later seven-year-old Daud declared 'Mami, your skin is getting darker like mine. If you drink lots of tea you'll get Indonesian skin!'

And Anne's own words? 'I am content that I am passing through this world en route for the Father's house. My citizenship is in heaven. The Word of God and the Blood of Jesus identify me with His people'.

Meanwhile, with all its ups and downs, frustrations, traumas and joys, life at Beth Shan went on.

Anne received a message from the Yayasan telling her that they had sanctioned the admission to Beth Shan of Untung, a tiny baby boy born out of wedlock. Already overstretched and exhausted Anne did not respond very well to this latest development. She was annoyed that she had not been consulted before a decision was made and inwardly began to rebel against the Yayasan and against God. Unaware of the emotional upheaval he had caused Untung arrived at Beth Shan, clearly very sick and with a skin infection covering his entire body. He would need a lot of nursing care.

On April 17th Anne flew with her mother to Jakarta, where they were able to spend a couple of relaxed days together before Dorothy Dakin's return flight to England.

On April 21st, with her mother safely en route for home, Anne flew from Jakarta to the island of Sumatra where she had been invited to join in a series of social gatherings and to give daily talks to the guests.

She attended a special service at Rumbai on the Saturday evening and the following morning made a two-and-a-half hour journey through the jungle to Duri where she led a very mixed congregation in worship. She based her thoughts on Psalm 40:8 where the Psalmist declares, 'I delight to do Your will, O my God, yea, Your law is within my heart,' unaware that before long she would be forcibly reminded of her own words. On Monday, before returning to Rumbai, she led a morning Bible Study, and many of the thoughts she shared on that occasion were a challenge to her own heart. On the flight back to Jakarta, flying over the vast jungle regions of Sumatra, she was very aware of God.

As she stepped off the plane at Solo Airport Audrey and a number of the children were there to welcome her, all talking at once as her luggage was loaded into the pick-up. She had taken with her to Sumatra 18 kilos of greetings cards, beautifully hand-painted by the older children, and had brought back in exchange an equivalent weight in good quality second-hand children's clothing. 'A new little boy has come, Mami,' the children told her excitedly, 'and he can't even talk.' 'In that case,' Anne whispered fiercely to Audrey, 'as I was not consulted Ayub and his wife can look after him.'

Ayub Lande was Anne's pastor and a member of the Yayasan, and after a hasty cup of tea at Beth Shan Anne left to visit him. She was quite determined as she strode along the track leading to Ayub's house. This really was too much and this time no-one would persuade her to change her mind – but that was before she heard Ayub's story.

The police had found the little boy, about four years old, wandering on the railway track, and at present they had no means of identifying him. He was deaf and unable to speak, and was partly paralysed down his left side. Would Beth Shan be willing to take him in while efforts were made to trace his family?

'My heart just went out to the little one,' Ayub concluded, 'He was so helpless and there was no-one at all to care for him'.

Anne felt chastened as she listened. In Sumatra she had spoken to others about delighting to do God's will, not just when it suits us but also when it does not, and now the Holy Spirit was ministering to her through her own words. She felt her body relax as anger and resentment disappeared.

At Beth Shan a family conference was called to decide what they should call their latest arrival. After all, every child must have a name! After much discussion they settled on Herri Setiawan – Herri for short!

Herri adapted very quickly to his new surroundings, walking around with his face wreathed in smiles and with eyes that communicated far too much!

Daily sports were started for the toddlers so that he could take part, and gradually he found exercise less painful. Arrangements were made for him to go each Thursday to a special training centre in Solo, together with Beth Shan's other disabled children.

Anne shuddered when she thought about the long-term implications, with endless visits to doctors and specialists, and perhaps the need to enrol him in the special school for the deaf where Yanto and Lidia were being educated.

Firmly Anne refused to project herself into the future; one step at a time was God's way and she had discovered long ago that His was the only way that worked.

A visit from the Welfare Department served as a reminder of problems and pressures outside Beth Shan. By law, Anne was told, second-hand clothing could no longer be received because of the threat of Aids. Knowing that Aids could not be contracted via clothing made no difference – the law was the law!

Robi was the next arrival. He was just twenty-seven days old and had been left at the local hospital labelled 'unwanted'. Before long he would discover that he was very much wanted at Beth Shan!

In the midst of all the busyness and confusion Kay Wilson, a friend from England arrived, and found herself at once caught up in the life of this very special family.

News came through that Joko's father had been traced; that he had remarried, and was now the father of six more children. Joko sobbed uncontrollably. He had previously suffered great cruelty at the hands of his stepmother, one result being the loss of the sight of one eye; and his longing to make contact with his father was mixed with a deep-seated fear.

The staff realised that great caution would be needed and knowing that there is nothing impossible with God they began to pray that both Joko's father and his stepmother would become Christians.

Elisa and Desianti were two lovely children who had come to Beth Shan in 1980 following the death of their father, and Anne was shocked when she received news of their mother's death.

She had been taken ill and admitted to hospital where cancer was diagnosed, but before any treatment could be started she had suddenly collapsed and died. 'If only I had known sooner,' Anne sighed, 'the girls could have been taken to visit her. Now it is too late.' At first the girls were inconsolable. They had loved their mother and she had loved them. Now they would never see her again. Anne did all she could to comfort and support them and a week later took them to visit her grave, a journey of some 70 kilometres out of town.

Agustunik had been at Beth Shan since she was just a year old, but now her mother had remarried and she was going home.

She had grown into a lively and happy eight-year-old and although tearful at first she gradually warmed to the prospect of returning to her own family. Her mother was given a Bible when she came to collect her and after two months news came through that Augustunik was settling well.

Lukas and Cap Sen both passed their exams and were thrilled when they were offered places at Solo University. They decided to move into digs near the campus but to return to Beth Shan each weekend so that they could maintain their links with the local church and continue to teach in Sunday School.

In the university and at their digs they found that most of their fellow students were Muslims and consequently the fellowship at weekends was very important to them.

With constant rain, staff shortages and a flu epidemic, September was not an easy month. As pressures mounted Anne found herself easily irritated and out of patience with the children, and she longed for a spirit of gentleness and laughter that would change her attitude.

Endang was suffering increasingly with sight problems, and when the specialist examined her he expressed grave concern about her condition. In mid-December she was admitted to hospital in Yogyakarta for emergency eye surgery and at the same time Yanto had an operation in Solo hospital. Nursing care in Indonesia is always a family responsibility and Anne's relief was great when both patients were well enough to return home.

On the national news Beth Shan learnt of the overthrow of communism in the countries of Eastern Europe and rejoiced with the rest of the free world.

With little time left to prepare for Christmas the children designed a mural for the hallway to illustrate the words 'Thanks be to God for His unspeakable Gift'. Two outstretched hands held a beautiful parcel with the name 'Jesus' written across it and the chosen text splashed above it. It was a simple Christmas with a service at the church followed by a meal of two savouries and steamed cake washed down with a glass of tea!

On December 26th, 1989, the family held a belated Thanksgiving Celebration and as a practical expression of their thanks to God for His faithfulness through another year they decided to mark the occasion with a love-offering.

The money given was used to buy Bibles for some of the people of Eastern Europe who wanted one so badly and had been denied one for so long.

Early in the New Year one hundred and twenty school children descended on Beth Shan for a somewhat belated Christmas celebration! Anne was determined that her response would be positive and took the opportunity to share with them the true meaning of Christmas. Once they had left the decorations were taken down and life returned to some degree of normality.

In spite of their continued struggles with deep emotional trauma Eko and Dani Kris were both showing signs of progress and a greater openness. Prahyuda was clearly responding to love and attention and as his vocabulary slowly increased the neurologist advised putting him into kindergarten school. Herri was learning to crawl in an effort to improve his balance and was doing well. Due to tuberculosis he was a year late starting school and although he had some difficulty in learning to lip read he was clearly a very bright child.

The law now stated that members of staff must attend a general meeting of orphanages each month and that two children should also be present. Beth Shan was the only Christian orphanage involved, with the rest arriving gowned and masked as their faith required. Every four months Beth Shan was responsible for hosting the session and on March 24th, 1990 a group of sixty duly arrived. Determined not to let an opportunity be lost Anne made sure that plenty of Scripture verses covered the walls and trusted the Holy Spirit to do the rest!

She organised a Ladies Retreat for Central Java from March 16th to 18th and took as her theme 'Listening to God'. The police asked for an outline of the programme and of the teaching involved and as she prepared Anne prayed that their eyes would be opened to the truth as they read.

Early in March twenty-five children and six members of staff went down with conjunctivitis and just as Anne was beginning to wonder if she would have to cancel her plans a small parcel from a friend in England arrived.

It contained a small phial of perfume attached to a piece of Cornish slate and written on the slate were words from the Song of Solomon, 'Come away, my Fair One'. Anne attended the Retreat and trusted God to watch over her family.

Sheila Few, from Andover in Hampshire, visited Beth Shan towards the end of March and Anne was glad to have her company and her friendship. The children welcomed her too – they could never have too many 'tantes', especially when they were prepared to share in their fun and games and Sheila quickly became their friend.

With Retti still away from the office May was a busy month, and with humidity high and temperatures well into the nineties even the smallest tasks were exhausting. The feast of Ramadan was almost over and Beth Shan received lots of Muslim visitors who came to pay their respects to the poor in order to 'earn' their salvation! Groups of Christians came too, eager to share in the Easter celebrations.

Anne coveted the blessings of an obedient life whatever the cost, but continued to struggle with self-pity and rebellion over her excessive workload. Coping with official papers in another language was particularly frustrating and time-consuming as the battle against fatigue went on.

Meilina became very ill with a high fever and caused great concern as a local epidemic of haemorrhagic fever continued to claim lives. Thankfully with careful nursing she pulled through and in the meantime fever and eye infections once again did the rounds.

Anne was becoming increasingly concerned about the office situation. Retti had already been away for nine weeks and had now written to say that she could not return for a further three months. With children needing to be enrolled in new schools it was a crucial time and created a lot of pressure. Retti was twenty-eight years old, unmarried and a Christian, living in a culture where singleness in women was seen as a stigma. Muslims added to the pressures as they were encouraged to marry Christian girls in order to convert them to Islam. It was a complex situation.

Officials came to evaluate the work being done at Beth Shan and complained that the staff were not attending their workshops; yet another reminder that political pressures were never far away.

Elisa, Ester and Endarwarti had all passed their exams and were now required to register for further education. They had reached a crucial stage in their young lives and the family prayed that God would show them clearly the path He wanted each of them to take.

Life was also proving difficult for Cap Sen and Li Sen. Their Chinese father, long deceased, had failed to register as an Indonesian and so was considered an alien and a possible part of the Communist faction that had attempted a coup. Their mother was illiterate and barely existing in very reduced circumstances. The boys needed to be naturalised but family papers had been lost in a fire and now the authorities were refusing to process new ones.

Anne realised that unless a solution could be found the boys would not be allowed to sit their final exams or obtain work and this became another matter for urgent prayer.

Kurniawan was now twenty-two years old and after sitting his final exams he was offered work in Kudus. With a four hour drive involved it was clear that he would need to find accommodation nearer to his work. Anne was thankful that although he remained very shy he was clearly growing in his walk with the Lord.

Sari qualified as a hairdresser and when she found work some distance away it was clear that she, too, must soon leave the nest. A new chapter was beginning in the life of the Beth Shan family.

Summer camps arranged for the teenagers were a great success with many of them sleeping under canvas for the first time. The days proved spiritually fruitful and Sab was among those who testified to God's fresh touch upon his life. Three weeks later he was baptized in the little village church where he had grown up.

Dani Kristianto remained very depressed and caused Anne deep concern. He knew that he had been rejected and it hurt. Other children knew that one of their parents was still alive although they never visited and the feelings of being unwanted and unloved refused to go away. Inevitably this affected schoolwork and many would carry deep scars all through their lives.

In August Anne travelled to Kediri Baptist Hospital in East Java where she was seen by a Dr. Duval who diagnosed depression due to exhaustion, and advised her to stop work.

He put her on hormone replacement therapy and she agreed to take three months out for a complete rest. When she returned to Beth Shan she was rested, but with temperatures reaching 120 degrees Fahrenheit she continued to find the humidity and extreme heat very trying.

When Sheila Few left to stay with friends in Australia Anne missed her company and the luxury of conversation in her mother tongue.

Ninil arrived to replace Retti in the office and Anne was able to lay down some of the administrative responsibilities she had carried for several months. Pak Sugiato had been Beth Shan's driver for several years but he had been less reliable of late and when he finally decided to leave the Yayasan found and appointed Pak Yono who was to prove a good man and a careful driver.

Endang and Kunyil were now in their twenties and their needs seemed to have outgrown what Beth Shan could offer. Would they now benefit more if transferred to a special school?

'Life seems to flow fairly smoothly at present in spite of all the demands', Anne wrote in a prayer letter to her supporters, 'until Jadid has a fit or Endang, without any provocation, flies off the handle and attacks a five-year-old, gripping her unfortunate victim around the neck.' Endang had just celebrated her 25th birthday and was becoming increasingly difficult to handle, with jealousy of the younger children making her very aggressive towards them.

These and other matters would require

careful thought and much prayer but in spite of the many causes for concern within the family there was much fun and laughter and visitors would often comment on the atmosphere of love that pervaded the home.

In November, as she looked back over another year now rapidly drawing to a close, Anne wrote, 'Sometimes loss of faith and a sense of panic causes us to lose our vision and the reality of the Lord's Presence, but we praise Him that He remains faithful even when we fail to recognise His work.'

At the end of 1990 there were fifty-two children living at Beth Shan.

11

1991 – 1996

Second storey completed.
Difficult days. A rescue.

Early in January 1991 Audrey Corser arrived for a long visit to the great delight of both children and staff. For Anne, suffering from total exhaustion and 'burnout', her coming was a lifeline and a demonstration of God's perfect timing. To converse in her mother-tongue, to unburden her heart to someone she knew would understand, and to have the benefit of Audrey's involvement as one of the family meant more than words could say.

Anne arranged a small celebration as a tribute to five of her staff who had worked with her at Beth Shan since 1981. Pak Timan and Sugiati were presented with a sewing machine, Pak and Ibu Mesdi with a lounge cabinet and Menik a wardrobe. They had all worked hard and shown great loyalty and it was good to have an opportunity to say 'terima kasih' – 'thank you' – in a practical way.

Several small tremors were felt locally as Mount Merapi, one of Java's most active volcanoes, became more active. Although some forty miles from Beth Shan it was clearly visible and enhanced the view across the roof-tops and rice paddies.

'It's Ramadan', Anne wrote in her March prayer letter, 'when all good Moslems fast from sunrise to sunset to gain favour with their Maker. The mosque blares a little louder and it's customary to attend a daily gathering to listen to the Koran. On April 16th, there will be a worldwide celebration.'

Indonesia declared Good Friday a public holiday 'out of respect for the Christian faith' and a television programme presented a clear gospel message without restrictions. In an unsettled and rapidly changing political situation there was still much to thank and praise God for.

Anne flew back to the U.K. on June 14th for a long-anticipated family reunion in Cornwall and an extended furlough. She knew that this break was vital to her health and that she was leaving her children in the safe hands of staff members who really cared about them. Letters from children as well as staff kept her in touch with all the ups and downs of life at Beth Shan and were a constant source of pleasure and encouragement. 'I hope your stay in England will be a delicacy,' wrote twelve-year-old Agus, clearly keen to master the English language!

Li Sen left for Surabaya to sit his entrance exams to train as an aviation engineer at the Aviation Engineering Training School. This had been his ambition for a long time and he wanted desperately to succeed.

Joko's father, prayed for so often, was admitted to hospital with advanced TB and died two days later. He had recently become a Christian and Joko had been able to visit the family on several occasions. His father's death left him with a great sense of responsibility towards his younger half-brothers and sisters and he continued to visit them regularly. He had now left school and was working on various projects at Beth Shan including the care and breeding of fish to sell.

There was encouraging growth at the little village church in Cemani and at the end of May fifteen young people were baptized, including Ruli, Li Sen, Agus, Elisa, Ester and Endwarti from the Beth Shan family. It was a time of great rejoicing with praise and glory offered to God by the whole congregation.

After a long period of total rest Anne attended a Christian Counselling Course at

Waverley Abbey Hall in Surrey. It was not an easy time as she struggled to concentrate on her studies and at the same time regain an awareness of God in her personal life. For so long she had longed to communicate with Him in a deeper way and was conscious of what she described as 'head knowledge that never made it to the heart'. Slowly the dreadful blackness began to lift as she confessed and repented of her independent spirit that had so often pushed God out. She brought to Him the resentment and the bitterness which were the outcome of many hurts and fears, asking for forgiveness. With that forgiveness came praise and a deeper awareness of the overflowing mercy and love of God that would never be denied her.

She returned to Beth Shan in November, feeling stronger and more relaxed but it was not long before she realised that life had not been without its traumas during her absence.

Many of the sixty children currently in her care were now in their late teens and with the inevitable problem of relationships the staff would need to be constantly on their guard. Firmness, wisdom and patience in abundance must be her daily prayer.

In March 1992 a new building project was launched at Beth Shan to complete the second storey and provide much needed additional space. Anne left for a three-week holiday in Nepal at the end of March staying with missionary friends John and Judith Bradley who were serving with the International Nepal Fellowship. It was her first visit to the country and it made a lasting impression on her. She was thrilled with its unique landscape, cultural diversity and its unforgettable people, to say nothing of a change of diet which included milk and cream from the water buffalo. 'Delicious,' Anne commented on her return!

At the end of April Joko, Munarsih (Snoos) and Lusi were baptized and she witnessed their public testimony with a thankful heart.

Joko was now very successful in rearing catfish, so much so that when the professionals lost all their stock it was to Joko they came for advice and help – and consequently offered him a job! How badly he needed some 'good things' to happen in his life

New children continued to arrive, many of them very young. February 5th saw the arrival of Andhi, a ten-year-old Chinese boy whose parents had divorced when he was four years old. His mother was now heavily involved in black magic and lived in a kiosk on the roadside. She worked as a prostitute and when 'clients' were expected Andhi was turned out on the streets where he got into bad company and began to steal. Damaged by rejection and by the evil influences that had touched his life he had a serious learning block and was admitted to a school for children with special learning problems.

He desperately needed love and understanding but his influence on the other children had to be closely monitored.

During March and April a total of seventy missionaries were asked to leave the country as clampdowns and unrest continued. 'Whatever the cost, Lord', Anne prayed, 'may the church in Indonesia rise to the challenge'. How thankful she was that she was now an Indonesian citizen.

The greetings cards project was now well established and was proving a great success, with good sales outlets in Sumatra, Salawesi, Jakarta and many other parts of the country.

1992 was proving a difficult year and revealed many things that Anne found it hard to come to terms with. Certainly her fears were confirmed with regard to the older teenagers who were still in her care. The greatest shock was the discovery that Cap Sen was the father of a two-year-old boy whose mother was Retti, the office worker who had left Beth Shan without an acceptable explanation three years earlier.

The affair finally came to light when Retti made contact with Beth Shan, demanding financial help in supporting the child, and the Yayasan moved quickly to take strong disciplinary action against Cap Sen.

All funding for his education and his day-to-day living costs were withdrawn and he was forced to sell milk at the roadside in order to survive. For Cap Sen, who had been part of the Beth Shan family since 1976 this was a 'deep tunnel' experience and Anne's heart ached for him.

She longed to offer practical help but knew it would be wrong to do so and confessed that she did not find it easy to forgive Retti. She had placed such confidence and trust in her and the fact that she was Cap Sen's senior by ten years made things even harder to come to terms with.

Anne knew that radical changes would have to be made at Beth Shan and she agreed with the Yayasan that the older teenage boys must all move into digs. To remain part of the Beth Shan family, which would continue to fund them, they would be expected to report home every one or two weeks depending on the distance involved. At least living out would give them a greater measure of independence and freedom and would involve them more in the local culture. The repercussions of this affair were far-reaching and would continue for a long time to come, but in spite of all the problems and heartache there was still much that gave Anne every right to feel proud of her older children.

Li Sen, Cap Sen's younger brother, was one of eleven finalists to pass his entrance exams and was accepted by Garuda Indonesian Airways for a three-year engineering course, while Li Min, their sister, left to begin work in West Java.

In spite of all his deep-seated emotional problems Anne became aware of a gradual change in Joko, and was overjoyed when he announced that he had received Jesus into his heart and life. Three weeks later he was baptized before leaving Beth Shan to begin work at a fish farm. He was the only Christian in the area but found a church in a nearby town which he attended regularly.

Anne's heart was full of praise to the Lord for all the healing Joko had received and his testimony served as a constant reminder that absolutely nothing is impossible with God.

Sabdinator and Ruli moved into digs in Solo where they were doing computer studies, while Paulus moved to Semarang to begin an apprenticeship in banking. Eko was also in

Semarang studying electronics, but although he was doing well he remained depressed over his family situation. He was the only Christian in a Muslim family and both his parents were blind. His real father had been killed while crossing the road and he had just discovered that his mother was going to divorce his stepfather. She planned to marry another blind man who already had a wife and family and the fact that she had not bothered to tell him what she was intending to do caused him a lot of distress.

Kurniawan was working in the administration section of a television electronics factory; his brother Lukas was at university studying agriculture and Eva, their older sister, had passed her nursing exams with high marks and was now working in East Java. Yes, Anne truly did have much cause to feel proud of her older children.

Seven-year-old Andre and seventeen-year-old Yogi were both admitted to hospital with haemorrhagic fever and were desperately ill. Working in shifts, members of staff stayed at their bedsides until the crisis point was passed and they were considered well enough to be nursed at home. At the same time a bout of flu was followed by rampant conjunctivitis and the sick bay was full.

It was at times like this that Anne was particularly aware of the dedication and loyalty of her staff, although staffing problems remained unpredictable. Within three days one staff member was knocked off her bicycle on her way home from work and had to be hospitalised, Pak Mesdi was admitted for surgery and a third went into hospital to give birth to her first child.

Anne received a message that Pastor Ayub and his wife Diana had been involved in an accident when an oncoming train caught the back of their motorbike and dragged them some distance before throwing them clear. Diana was admitted to hospital with a fractured pelvis but amazingly they both escaped without serious injury. Anne was thankful for the help of her older girls as they took it in turns to keep a vigil at Diana's bedside.

With the arrival of three more children, Supri, Joko Waluyo and Lidia, Anne was thankful that her staff were working well and all pulling together. Ten years earlier a little boy named Danang had been admitted to Beth Shan and sadly had died, but as a result of his death his parents became Christians and decided to build a church in their village. Ten-year-old Lidia, one of the new arrivals, came from the same village, and as a result of the

184

witness of Danang's parents her own parents had turned to the Lord. How amazing is God's weaving together the threads of individual lives! The family lived in great poverty with hardly enough money for food and none for schooling.

Her father had died three months ago and overwhelmed with grief her mother died a month later, leaving behind five orphaned children. The sight of this tragic little girl brought tears to Anne's eyes. She was very thin with skin like coarse sandpaper and bald patches on her head due to malnutrition. There was a deep sadness in her eyes and she could barely talk.

Following the death of the parents all five children had one by one gone down with typhoid and two did not recover. Sri Suwarni, Lidia's older sister, was hospitalised with Beth Shan stepping in to help with the hospital fees. At first she was not expected to live but following a blood transfusion she gradually gained strength and when she was well enough to leave hospital she joined Lidia at Beth Shan. She looked about thirteen years old and Anne was shocked to learn that she was actually seventeen.

Decisions would have to be made about her future but for the moment she needed love and nourishment. Lidia's delight at having her sister close by was lovely to see and was bound to play a part in her own progress.

For the first time the children were invited to join in the local celebrations for Independence Day and Anne was delighted. They danced and sang in a concert giving an excellent performance and she was justly proud of them all. She knew that this involvement with the local community was vitally important and she had waited for eighteen years for it to happen!

Li Sen was thrilled when, as a result of his hard work and high grades, Garuda Airways sent him to university. Cap Sen now visited Beth Shan quite often and was gradually becoming more like his old self. Li Min had offered to help with his expenses which meant that he was able to continue with his university studies.

At Beth Shan there was much to encourage and be thankful for, although the problems of lying, absconding and stealing seemed to be never far away, sometimes involving members of staff as well as children.

Anne described Christmas 1993 as 'the best ever' with the staff going from room to room early on Christmas morning singing carols to awaken the children. Later, at family worship, there was a lump in her throat as she studied their happy faces. 'O come, let us adore Him'

– their voices echoed through the building on a day that was full of laughter and rejoicing.

No, she had certainly not realised the implications of her response to Len Moules' appeal in Redruth Methodist Church so many years before but at moments like this she was very thankful that she had been obedient to God's call. 'Terima Kasih, Bapa', she whispered in her heart.

Early in 1994 there was great sadness at Beth Shan when Sutrisno, severely disabled through cerebral palsy, died in hospital. He had been part of the family for fifteen years and now at last he was free of all his suffering and limitations.

Caring for his constant needs had been tiring both physically and emotionally, but he would always keep his special place within the family and both staff and children knew how much they would miss him. The funeral service was held at Beth Shan with many local folk joining with the family. The Javanese have a saying 'gone home to his Father's lap' which describes so beautifully the death of a child like Sutrisno.

The following week, in accordance with Javanese custom, a Service of Thanksgiving for his short life was held. During his last weeks in hospital members of Beth Shan staff had kept a constant vigil by his bedside, and exhausting though those weeks may have been, it was good to come together to praise God and to thank Him for all that they had learnt, often without realising it, from Sutrisno. And now there was Jadid, also suffering from cerebral palsy; Endang and Kunyil, and several others learning to cope with various disabilities. They each had particular needs and also had much to teach those who cared for them.

It was Easter 1994 when Anne set out with twenty-three teenagers for a three-day camping holiday, heading for a small cove in East Java about fifteen miles from Pacitan Bay. Rocks and strong currents made swimming impossible but as the youngsters could enjoy fishing at low tide it would still be a time of fun and recreation.

Tukimin was paddling in very shallow water when he began to get into difficulties and when Gehu ran to help him a huge wave claimed his inner tube and he was dragged away by the current. Yogi, tall and strong, tried to reach them both but quickly got into difficulties himself.

Anne recorded the events that followed – 'Horrified, I ran to the scene where villagers had already gathered. The other teenagers were crying on the beach and we could hardly see the boys because of the size of the waves. The villagers told us that there was no hope as we began to pray and call out to God. As I waited on the beach I felt so small and helpless and incapable. Within minutes Yogi was suddenly enveloped by a huge wave and carried in another direction right up to the beach and as it were 'vomited on to dry land'! As I stood straining to locate Gehu and Tukimin two dugout fishing boats literally skimmed across the waves paddling furiously, and I'm sure with the aid of an Unseen Hand. Suddenly I saw a big Cross on the horizon and as the fishermen rescued Gehu and Tukimin the words of Romans 8 flashed through my mind – 'While you were helpless and powerless God sent Jesus to die for you.' The reality of God's rescue plan for a lost world, for me, hit home as I watched those two men risk their lives for my boys.'

As they approached shore Tukimin was sitting up but there was no sign of Gehu who was lying down in the boat and was in quite a bad way. He had swallowed a lot of sea water and another twenty-four hours passed before he was well enough to join in any further activities.

With the youngsters now safe the family

went to each cove for a time of prayer and thanksgiving, and Anne wondered how many of the local villagers were hearing about the love of Jesus for the first time. She prayed that God would show them how to maintain contact and how to communicate to these needy people the message of God's love.

The following Sunday in church Yogi gave a very moving testimony as he relived those moments. He shared how he had realised that he might die and told God he was ready, but promising that if his life was spared he would commit himself fully to His service. Out of near tragedy God had brought tremendous blessing.

Across Indonesia there was a tangible uncertainty on every side and many people were turning to the Lord. How much longer would religious freedom survive as the clampdowns, cutbacks and expulsions continued? Christians were still being imprisoned and churches destroyed by fire. Permission to rebuild had to come from the Head of Department of Religion and so far not one permit had been granted.

Anne was delighted when after nearly ten years of waiting a telephone was installed while at the same time questions about the future of Beth Shan and about her own future chased themselves around in her mind. Repeatedly

190

words from the first chapter of Deuteronomy came to her – 'You have been in the place long enough; get up and go up'. These were not easy days.

For seven months workmen had been completing the building of the second storey at Beth Shan and at last, towards the end of February 1995, the work was finished! It was good to be free of noise and dust at last and to have proper sleeping space for children who had been overcrowded for so long. All the same, with a further ten children having joined the family since September 1994, there was a distinct possibility that before long Beth Shan would once again be bursting at the seams!

Among the new arrivals was Taukhid aged three years and two-year-old Dwi, joining Andhi, their half-brother; Ferry, an orphaned eight-year-old, Gessa and Anisa aged three years and eighteen months respectively, ten-year-old Supri, and Kristiawati, an orphaned girl of thirteen years whose grandmother was now too old to care for her. Beth Shan certainly needed that completed second storey!

A six-week furlough from mid-April to the end of May gave Anne brief but welcome relief from the daily demands upon her physical and emotional strength.

The time passed all too quickly and on her

return she was plunged once more into all the ups and downs of life with her large family.

As 1995 moved towards its close her thoughts drifted back over twenty truly remarkable years. She remembered the little house at Baron where Tutik had come as her first helper and where Adi had been welcomed as Beth Shan's first child.

She had lost count of the number of children who had passed through her hands since those early days, all of them with scarred lives, and of the parents whose grief and heartache she had shared and whose pain had so often become her own. The kindergarten school had been built and together with the village church continued to forge strong links between Beth Shan and the local community. The Retreat Centre at Kopeng, surrounded by such beautiful mountain scenery, was now a place used by many seeking time apart with God. When it was time to leave most spoke of feeling refreshed and renewed and ready to resume the particular work that God had called them to.

She thought about the helpers who had worked with her over the years, many of them now so much a part of the Beth Shan family; and of the times of crisis and panic, of celebration and thanksgiving, now too numerous to recall. What amazing things she had seen and learnt and how faithful God had been all through those years. And what of the future? She was content to leave it with God.

During her stay at Beth Shan Audrey Corser (now Audrey Mann) had set up 'LINK CHILD', with the specific purpose of gaining prayer partners for each child. She and Anne both recognised the value of individual love and attention and above all regular and informed prayer support. Although there was no financial commitment involved many who became prayer partners chose to write to the child they were supporting and a letter addressed to a child personally never failed to cause great excitement and delight. Anne valued this special ministry to her children especially as numbers continued to grow and limited the amount of individual attention she could give.

In April 1996 Anne left Indonesia to attend a conference in Australia which proved to be a time of great encouragement and blessing. It was good, however, when it was time to return to her family where change seemed to be the order of the day.

Three children left to return to their families and during the summer three new children and a four-month-old baby arrived.

Eleven-year-old Hannes and his younger

brother, Andre, became quite unmanageable and were having such a bad influence on the other children that after much prayer and heart-searching Anne knew that she could no longer keep them at Beth Shan. They had been with her for ten years and it was a painful decision to make. They were returned to the care of their mother who was comforted by promises of help and support whenever possible.

Even sadder was the parting with ten-year-old Maria who was forced to return to her family home where Anne knew she would be subject to abuse and possible prostitution. She hated having to let her go and could only pray that what she had learned about Jesus would help her in the hard times ahead.

But there was good news too! On July 9th, Limin gave birth to a lovely baby girl and Anne revelled in the fact that she was now a grandmother!

Anne attended a special ceremony with Lukas to request the hand of Dewi in marriage. Lukas had to be very careful in his approach as Dewi, a lovely girl, had received much family opposition to her Christian faith, but the evening went well and a possible wedding date later in the year was discussed.

News came from Sabdinator (Sab) who had been sent back to his pastor in Kalimantan three years ago and had drifted far from God. Now, with renewed faith, he was trekking for miles every day in the outback, sharing the good news about Jesus at every opportunity. He announced that he hoped to be accepted for a two-year course at Bible School later in the year. In spite of all the setbacks what a lot there was to praise God for!

Andhi continued to cause problems, constantly running away from Beth Shan and often truanting from school. On one occasion he found his way back to his mother's house but she did not want him and turned him out on the streets. When he arrived back Anne warned him that if he ran away again he would not be allowed to return.

She gave him a document to sign which listed the 'ground rules' to be obeyed if he wanted to stay. To her great surprise he not only signed the document but his behaviour noticeably improved too. Maybe he was going to settle down at last!

Sheila Few visited Beth Shan again in July 1996 and both staff and children were pleased to see her again. As the year progressed the older children were busy making cards and handicrafts to sell at various markets with further outlets opening up in Jakarta and Sumatra. With profits from sales going towards the children's education costs and also providing the occasional treat, the results were very encouraging.

Sheila decided to remain over the Christmas period and looked forward to sharing in the family celebrations. Sixteen of the children formed a choir and were invited to sing three times each week during December at the new Sheraton Hotel in Solo. They made a great impression and were booked to sing again the following Easter. With no restrictions on their choice of songs they were thrilled to have the opportunity to share the gospel message with so many different groups of people.

Christmas 1996 was a wonderful time of celebration with the familiar songs and carols welcoming the coming of the Prince of Peace but outside Beth Shan the atmosphere was very different as tension and a sense of foreboding grew stronger.

Anne knew that whatever lay ahead God had promised that He would ever remain the refuge and strength of His people.

12

1997 – 1998

Unrest in Indonesia.
An evacuation and a wedding.

1997 dawned without incident. On the surface all appeared calm but underneath unrest and discontent silently simmered. Troops and police guarded all routes into Solo as rumours of an uprising increased.

Warnings were circulated that mobs were threatening to go on the rampage, setting fire to buildings as they went. A date was given when the riots would begin and the decision was taken to evacuate Beth Shan. Groups of people in many places in Indonesia and far beyond came together to pray and as the chosen day dawned it rained in Solo as it had never rained before! Very little could burn after such a continuous dowsing! With the military guarding the city and the angels of the Lord guarding Beth Shan the day passed without event.

Gradually the family trickled back and in

spite of everything the wedding of Lukas and Dewi went ahead as planned. They were married in Cemani church, in the village where Lukas had grown up as part of the Beth Shan family, a happy couple and very much in love. It was a day of great celebration and a wonderful opportunity to praise and thank God for all His goodness, mercy and protection.

As the situation calmed down locally life at Beth Shan returned to some degree of normality, but the family remained on alert, packed and ready to evacuate quickly should the need arise.

At the beginning of April Anne returned home for a short visit. She felt the need to spend time with her family and particularly to be with her mother who had felt the strain of recent events so deeply.

It was not easy to leave her children even for a short break but Anne realised her own need to come apart and rest after all the trauma of recent months. It also gave her the opportunity to visit America where she enjoyed a family wedding celebration. She returned to Beth Shan early in June refreshed and ready to take up once more the reins of responsibility for her large family.

Holiday time came round again and the family spent many happy days at Kopeng in perfect weather. The mountains, hills and valleys were breathtaking in their beauty and in the garden wild poinsettia trees created a wonderful blaze of colour.

With the end of another school year Lidia, Natalia and Emelia prepared to move on to Junior High School having successfully passed their eleven plus exams, while Daud and Setyo left school to continue their studies at a local technical college.

Sri Suwarni was now at Bible School, training for work in village evangelism, and during holiday times she enjoyed being back with the family and helping with the younger children.

Sabdinator (Sab) was also doing well at Bible School in Kalimantan and between studies was trekking through the rain forests to share with those previously unreached the message of the Gospel.

Wartini was a Christian and was under pressure to get married. She had been a member of staff at Beth Shan for fifteen years looking after the babies and toddlers, and was very happy in her work. There were tearful farewells at the end of July when she left to return to her Muslim family, vowing that when she did marry it would be to a Christian.

Early in July six-week-old En Dah joined the family and soon made her presence felt as she slept all day and cried incessantly through the night. With much vocal support from ten-month-old Putera Topan, three-month-old Jabes and Puteri, a little girl of almost three months, it was as if a contest was on to 'out-yell' one another! Pressures and demands were ever present and Anne struggled to maintain a close walk with God as she waged a constant war with busyness and fatigue.

And still the family grew – with the addition of two ducks, two chickens, five rabbits (plus families!), two guinea pigs and three white mice!

With staff needs continuing to fluctuate several of the youngsters now at college helped out at Beth Shan during their holidays and also continued to produce exquisite craft work to raise much-needed funds. Three more students were due to graduate later in the year and Anne felt a just pride in the individual achievements of all her children in spite of the pain and trauma that had so deeply scarred their lives.

Towards the end of November 1997 five new children arrived within a week, ranging in age from two days to eleven years, all of them unwanted and some the victims of ill-treatment and abuse. The number of children currently in Anne's care had now reached sixty.

Herri, who had joined the family in 1989,

was now fourteen years old and coping well in spite of his disabilities. He was clearly an intelligent boy and was learning to lip read.

Dani Kristianto was married in November and Anne was pleased to be there to share in the celebrations. What a host of recollections came flooding back as she looked at a very happy Dani with his lovely bride.

For most of November Anne was in Jakarta selling cards and crafts and speaking on a number of occasions. The art work of the children was quite professional and sales were encouraging, and when Anne returned to Beth Shan at the end of the month she felt that it had been a worthwhile trip both financially and spiritually.

The country was now facing its biggest crisis in thirty years with food scarce and shop shelves empty. Cooking oil was often unobtainable and packets of milk for baby feeds in very limited supply. The family continued to praise God for His faithfulness and provision and at Christmas unexpected gifts of rice (1,200 kilos) sugar (100 kilos), and green beans were thankfully received.

Faithfully Anne set aside one tenth of all that she received, distributing it among the needy village folk around Beth Shan. Several days of torrential rain caused serious flooding and every effort was made to protect the grain from getting wet and mouldy.

Because of continued threats to riot Solo remained under police protection with feelings of unease and apprehension almost tangible and at Beth Shan plans to evacuate at short notice remained in place.

Sheila Few arrived in Jakarta at the end of January 1998 into what was clearly a grave political situation. Food was very scarce and many families were forced to go hungry. Prices had rocketed and many basic items were not available in the shops. Police and military forces were everywhere and fear was in the air.

On May 12th, U.F.M. received an urgent fax from Anne as the situation in the area worsened. Many buildings in Solo had been set alight with Chinese-owned properties the main target. Shops, banks and many other buildings were destroyed and many lives were lost. Sheila Few and Sarah Callow, both visitors at Beth Shan were at particular risk as non-nationals. Anne ended her message with the words from the Book of Proverbs (18:10): 'The Name of the Lord is a strong tower.'

On Wednesday, May 20th, Sheila and Sarah were evacuated direct from Solo to Singapore en route for home. Being forced to leave Anne alone with the children in such a desperate situation was very difficult, and with other ex-patriots also on their way out of the country Anne was left with a strange feeling of isolation. 'He who dwells in the secret place of the most High shall abide under the shadow of the Almighty.' The familiar words of Psalm 91 helped to restore her peace.

Sir Robin Christopher, British Ambassador in Jakarta, was in regular contact with Anne and did all he could to ensure the safety of both children and staff and Anne was very thankful for his advice and support. With his wife he had previously visited Beth Shan and had been very impressed with the happy family atmosphere he found there. He had spent time chatting with the children and was visibly moved when they sang for their important visitors, giving of their best.

By May 22nd, the roads into Solo were open again and the children returned to school. Food was now very scarce and baby milk almost unobtainable but Anne praised God that she had felt prompted to go and do a 'big shop' the day before, especially as she had now been advised to remain indoors.

Although many local people sought shelter at Beth Shan, the Yayasan deemed it unwise and refused, apart from admitting one Muslim mother who was nine months pregnant and had nowhere to go. At night men from the village joined the older boys from Beth Shan in guarding the village and the orphanage from any possible intruders.

The following is an extract from a letter received from Anne in June 1998: 'Familiar haunts and shopping centres in Solo no longer exist. On May 14th–15th, 1998 Solo burned.

'75% of all businesses were destroyed.

'For ten days we were confined to Beth Shan, uncertain of what was happening on our doorstep.

'The repercussions of these events remain.

'Thousands are unemployed and there is no welfare state to help with debts, schooling fees etc.

'The cost of living rocketed and food became very scarce.

'Through 1998 provision for Beth Shan continued. The main diet of rice was bought for the staff and all the children's needs were met – often in unexpected ways. There were constant reminders that God's timing in these matters is always perfect.

'As rice stocks depleted within the nation we decided to save one kilo per day in case of urgent need.

'Two of the children decided to eat a spoonful of raw rice grain less per day and any change from housekeeping money was also set aside. In this way we created a simple method to give help to the poor and the youngsters at college and university rose to the challenge as they took on the responsibility of distributing our gifts.'

Anne was thankful that during the school holidays in July she was able to take the younger children to Kopeng for a holiday, and later to go camping with the teenagers, on both occasions leaving the college students at home to guard the house.

In August 1998 Anne was able to return to the U.K. for a short visit and was particularly anxious to spend time with her mother. Seeing the supermarket shelves stacked high with such a variety of goods was quite a culture shock after the empty shops and hungry families she had left behind in Solo.

Within Beth Shan there were many changes under way as Anne left for her home visit. Munarsih was studying for her Masters degree and decided to move out but would come home as often as possible to help with cards and craft-work. Desianti left to begin three months job training in Hotel and Catering and her sister Elisa moved to Jakarta in search of work there.

Early in June Dani Kurniawan married a girl who had converted to Christianity during their courting days and Anne prayed that their stand for the Lord would be strong and clear.

She was also deeply concerned about her own role as a member of the Yayasan, aware of the need for her position to be clarified and reviewed. It was a situation that called for much prayer.

In October the children's choir was again invited to sing at the Sheraton Hotel producing their own Christmas programme, singing on Christmas Eve and Christmas Day. They were very thrilled.

God continued to provide for the family and Anne realised she had not needed to buy any rice since December 1997!

In Solo and Cemani village many were living below the poverty line and tension in the area remained high. A Christian rally was planned for October 26th in the huge Solo Stadium, a reminder that God was still at work in spite of the tension and fear that gripped the lives of local people.

By November, however, the situation again gave cause for great concern with more rumours of riots circulating and schools closed, and again Anne contacted U.F.M. to make known the urgent need for prayer support. The situation remained critical as the year drew to its close. The deepening financial crisis within the country resulted in many more people losing their jobs and thus the means to feed and support their families. Anne knew that the future, whatever it might hold, was in God's hands.

13

1999

Celebrating twenty-five years.
Further unrest.

As 1999 dawned, in spite of the general feeling
of unease and uncertainty throughout
Indonesia, Anne did all she could to maintain
some degree of normality in the daily life of
Beth Shan. In Solo a certain amount of repair
work had begun but the main part of the city
lay in ruins.

March brought great sadness to the family
when Kunyil died in the Intensive Care Unit
of the local hospital. She had been unwell for
some time with a high fever and frequent
epileptic attacks. She was admitted on March
14th, and on the 21st passed into the Lord's
presence. Kunyil had been at Beth Shan since
1983 and had quickly established her own place
within the family and would be sadly missed.
She was a severe epileptic with the I.Q. of a
three-year-old and maybe it was her serious
disabilities that gave both children and staff a

special love for her. Her funeral service was held the following day with a large number of the village folk hearing the message of the gospel as they joined with the family to bid her farewell.

Desianti came home for an overnight visit having just completed the first six months of a two-year course at Bible College. She shared with Anne the great burden God had given her for the village of Bantul, a very impoverished area about three hours' drive from Beth Shan.

She longed to live there amongst the people and to share with them the message of Jesus, the Saviour, Healer and Deliverer. It was here that her elderly grandmother still lived and Desianti had only recently learnt from her that she had been practising as a witchdoctor for many years and that her love for her daughter, Desianti's mother, had turned to hatred when she became a Christian and went to Bible School. Desianti knew that if God confirmed her call she would need the backing of the church and an understanding of how to engage in spiritual warfare.

Elisa, her sister, had left Beth Shan in 1998 in a state of anger and deep distress, severing all links with Desianti and the rest of the family. Although there was currently no news of her many continued to pray for her safe return and for the healing of broken relationships.

Li Sen was made redundant after working for three years for Garuda Indonesian Airways and realised that with his Chinese origins he faced an uncertain future.

Elections were due to take place in Indonesia on June 7th, and tension increased again when it was planned that Megawati, leader of the opposition party, would visit Solo on June 3rd. Shutters were fixed on shop fronts and every precaution was taken to safeguard properties as the possibility of riots and demonstrations grew. Across the world many Christians were praying and the day passed without any serious problems.

Schools were closed because of the elections and with the family's car in need of major repairs the children were confined to the house. With riots still a possibility, Anne decided it was too risky to take the children out but coping with their pent-up energy indoors was not easy. It was with great relief that she waved them off to school on the morning of June 14th.

A measure of optimism was abroad with the election of Wahid, a moderate and respected man as president, and Megawati as vice-president, although the people were aware that the country's problems were far from over.

Stealing within Beth Shan was an ongoing

problem that was not easy to resolve. Anne knew that its roots lay in the backgrounds and situations from which many of the children had come. Ferry was a classic example. Following the death of both his parents at an early age a couple had adopted him. He gradually began to settle down until some time later his adoptive father also died, leaving his mother to earn enough money to support them both. She set up a street stall selling noodle soup but while she worked Ferry was left to his own devices. He became experienced at shoplifting and as a pickpocket and was brought to Beth Shan from the streets of Jakarta. His mother did not visit him or make any contact, and knowing she had rejected him his unhappiness found expression as he began to steal anything that caught his eye.

Many of the children had been studying hard for their exams and when the results came through they were for the most part good and encouraging. With several of the older boys moving into digs to continue their studies prior to graduating Anne was very aware that a new chapter was emerging in the life of Beth Shan.

A general meeting of the Yayasan was called for March 6th, 1999 with many important items on the agenda. With the establishing of various projects under the umbrella of Beth Shan, including the Retreat Centre at Kopeng, the Kindergarten School in Cemani village and more recently a Battered Wives Refuge close to the village church, Pontas Pardede (Chairman) was keen to introduce new structures. He advised the appointing of an 'Intermediary Board' to liaise between the Yayasan and these projects. No decisions were reached at the meeting but clearly the wind of change was blowing upon the work of Beth Shan Orphanage and Anne was reminded again of the need for her own role to be clarified.

Before long many friends would be arriving as the preparations began for the celebration of Beth Shan's 25th anniversary, with a reunion of family members past and present.

At the end of July Anne visited Kalimantan (Borneo) to attend Sab's graduation from Bible College taking Agus with her.

It meant so much to Sab that 'Mami' should be there for his special day, and for Anne the occasion filled her heart with joy as she recognised how deeply God had transformed his life.

Later they flew by M.A.F. (Mission Aviation Fellowship) plane into the interior to visit the Dyak tribe from which he had come to Beth Shan in 1976. Now he was working amongst them as an Assemblies of God pastor and already eight had responded to the message of the gospel. Sab baptised each of them as they publicly gave testimony to their new-found faith and transformed lives.

On August 28th, 1999, past and present members of the Beth Shan family and some of their closest friends came together in an atmosphere of joy and thanksgiving to celebrate Beth Shan's twenty-fifth anniversary. Sab was there, thrilled to be back after an absence of six years and delighted to renew contact with those with whom he had shared his childhood years.

Munarsih was there, now a beautiful young woman, with a Masters degree in pharmaceutical chemistry and a good job, and with a great love for Jesus in her heart. Cap Sen with his wife and small son, Limin with her husband Joshua and their three-year-old daughter, and Yanto and Lidia with their mother who had never lost touch with them through all the painful years of separation, they had all come to Beth Shan at the little house in Baron and a close bond existed between them.

Agus was there, brought to Beth Shan in 1976 aged just three days and now a fine young man and totally committed to God; together with Joko, Petrus, Sri Suwarni and many others who were now making their own way in the world. Under Anne's care they had found love and healing and discovered how important and special they were to God. So many memories were stirred as Anne gazed around at them all.

There were visitors from England, too, including Bill McIlroy, David and Sally Harlow and Sheila Few; each with a special place in Anne's life and in the story of Beth Shan. For each of them it was a great thrill to be there to share in the celebrations.

The Beth Shan children's choir, dressed in their choir uniforms sang for the guests, ending with the 'blessing song' in English as a prayer for Li Sen and Ester who that day were celebrating their engagement. 'May the blessing of the Lord our God rest upon you day by day. May He keep and guide you every step of the way. May you know He is with you, deep within your hearts, and may you know His joy in all you do and say.'

Li Sen and Ester had both grown up in Beth Shan and as teenagers had committed their lives to Jesus Christ. Their greatest desire was to ask for God's blessing upon their future years together and at their request, Ayub Lande, pastor of the Cemani church and a member of the Yayasan, conducted the engagement ceremony.

It was a beautiful and deeply moving occasion, especially for Anne who had watched them develop through their growing up years.

The refreshments which followed were special celebration fare beautifully presented and with a huge iced anniversary cake.

Next came a great time of entertainment, with sketches, singing and much laughter. Anne would always be 'Mami' to her children; the name given to her by Cap Sen in 1976 when he was just three years old, and her spiritual influence upon their lives could not possibly be measured. She had loved and cared for them and disciplined them too; listened to them and often wept with them as the process of healing began in their deeply traumatised lives. And always she had introduced them to Jesus Christ, who had died to save them, and had promised never to reject or abandon them. As she gazed around at them all on that very special day, some now with marriage partners and children of their own, Anne realised how much they in turn had enriched her own life. The going had often been very tough and at times she had been tempted to despair, but today she saw so clearly how worth while it had all been.

Indonesia had changed almost beyond recognition since she first arrived there in 1972 but although the future was unpredictable and uncertain she knew that she belonged to Indonesia and its people. For the future as for the past she was prepared to trust God and His Word, with the words of Psalm 91 always there in her heart to uphold and support her.

When the anniversary day was over the celebrations continued for the college students with a five-day trip to Lambok and Bali with Sheila Few and David and Sally Harlow joining them for a great time of fun and relaxation. Sab was there too, and for him it was a particularly precious time.

On September 18th, Sab left Beth Shan to return to Kalimantan where he would continue to serve God as pastor to his own people. Already he had a congregation of fifteen and planned on his return to build a church where they could meet together for worship and prayer. Although its location was deep in the rain forest and a six-hour boat ride from the nearest town he knew that with God on his side there was nothing to fear. Agus travelled with him to spend a month helping and supporting him in his work. Anne sent him on his way with plenty of new clothes and some strong shoes, and as he said his farewells he knew that the love and prayers of all the Beth Shan family went with him.

During September an uneasy peace settled

over Solo. News filtered through of violence in many of Indonesia's islands with villages destroyed and many lives lost. Early in November Anne was asked if she could provide shelter for a number of refugee children who had been made homeless when their villages were targeted. Twenty-three arrived on November 11th, most of them having lost family members and witnessed dreadful atrocities. They were undernourished and in poor health and all deeply traumatised.

How thankful Anne was for her older youngsters who rallied round to help in any way they could. In her November prayer letter she wrote 'As I surveyed the new faces, the sadness, confusion and bewilderment, all I could do was voice the Name of Jesus as the tears flowed freely. How could I undertake such a task when we were already stretched? Praise God for Psalm 138 and in particular verse 3. The Indonesian rendering is roughly 'He gives me all I need and goes on filling me and adding when the supply gets low'.'

There was much to be done practically, with school uniforms and shoes to buy, plus the need of a school prepared to accept so many children midterm with no educational background information to help.

In spite of all the upheaval Anne involved

the family in starting to prepare for Christmas with 'My heart is Your manger' as their chosen theme for 1999, and she was delighted when the children's choir was invited to sing for three hours on six occasions in the foyer of the Quality Inn Hotel in Solo.

Even as she was considering how they would cater for such a large family a group of people arrived at Beth Shan with the food left over from a wedding feast!

Some of it she stored in the freezer for a Christmas dinner.

14

2000

A new millennium.
More refugees. Family grief.

Early in January 2000 Anne was warned that there were further threats of violence in Solo and she was advised to evacuate Beth Shan. On January 18th, a well prepared plan was put into operation and between 8.30 p.m. and 3.30 a.m. the children were moved out in small groups to various locations. There was much prayer offered in many parts of the world and two days later they all returned safely to Beth Shan.

For the refugee children in particular it was a very frightening experience. On January 22nd, ten more children arrived having lost everything they possessed when their villages were burned to the ground.

Anne was now responsible for 93 children and the demands on her both physically and emotionally were enormous. A friend, Elspeth Rodrick, was visiting Beth Shan at this time and Anne was very thankful for her support and help. How accurate always is God's timing.

With the situation so volatile Anne arranged for the refugee children to be transported to and from school and was very relieved that the school was still prepared to accept them.

In spite of the added tension and extreme fatigue the already depleted Beth Shan staff battled on.

It was a particularly difficult time for Pak Timan and Sugiati with the added burden of caring for their son who was at home recovering from surgery for an infected appendix. He still required a lot of nursing care and hanging over them was a hospital bill they did not have the funds to meet.

On February 10th, Jadid died. He was sixteen years old and dearly loved by all the family. He had been born with severe cerebral palsy and was totally dependant on others for all his needs. Now, freed from all those limitations he, like Sutrisno before him, was 'gone home to his Father's lap'. He had been at Beth Shan since 1983 and it would seem strange without him.

Anne's mind flashed back to Daphne Chapman's two separate six-month visits. She had gone to Beth Shan primarily to sew and to lend a hand wherever there was a need and was in her element caring for Jadid and Sutrisno. Although they were unable to express their thanks verbally they clearly responded to her devoted love and dedicated care.

And what of the future?

Who will continue to lead and guide the work when Anne retires?

What changes will be needed in a vastly changing country?

What will be the future role of the Yayasan (Foundation Trust) and who will serve as its members?

Who does God have on His heart with the initiative and the vision to carry Beth Shan into the future?

In retirement will she remain in the country which was now her home? If so, where will she live?

How often Anne had pondered these questions in recent months.

She was aware that changes were inevitable, both in her own life and in the life of Beth Shan, but for the present she would remain with her family, trusting God for physical and emotional stamina sufficient for each day.

In the quietness of her heart she recalled another question, asked by Len Moules in Redruth, Cornwall, so many years ago.

'Is there anyone here tonight who is willing to go anywhere at any time for God?'

And the answer? 'In the silence which followed a young girl rose from her seat.'

In the Queen's birthday honours list in June 2000 Anne Dakin was awarded the M.B.E. for 'services to the community in Indonesia'.

Anne sums up her feelings about her life in Indonesia with all its challenges and testings with words from Psalm 66.

'You have purified us with fire, O Lord, like silver in a crucible. You captured us in Your net and laid great burdens on our backs. You sent troops to ride across our broken bodies. We went through fire and flood but in the end You brought us into wealth and great abundance. Now I have come to Your temple with burnt offerings to pay my vows....

'Come and hear, all you who reverence the Lord, and I will tell you what He did for me. For I cried unto Him for help, with praises ready on my tongue. He would not have listened if I had not confessed my sins. But He listened! He heard my prayer! He paid attention to it! Blessed be God who didn't turn away when I was praying, and didn't refuse me His kindness and love.'

'Take Your glory, Lord!

STATISTICS AND FAMILY NEWS 1998

Since Beth Shan opened its door and its heart to Indonesia's children in 1975 approximately 150 children have been welcomed for varying periods of time.

In 1998, 61 children are currently being cared for

36 more have now left
6 came for temporary help
20 have been adopted
4 have died
7 have married
and roughly 16 are unaccounted for

Many children and young people have become Christians during their years at Beth Shan and a number have been baptized at their local village church in Cemani.

Some who have now left Beth Shan are in full-time service for the Lord.

We give thanks to God for each one and covet for them the prayers of all who have read this book.

These statistics were researched at the end of 1998. Since then there has been a dramatic increase in the numbers of children admitted. Kunyil and Jadid have died and five more have married. Anne now has fifteen 'grandchildren' who are a special source of joy to her.

BETH SHAN'S EARLIEST CHILDREN – SOME UPDATES

MUNARSIH

Munarsih (Snoos) will be 26 years old on September 12th, 2000. She is a beautiful young woman and a committed Christian. She was Beth Shan's third child arriving on October 14th, 1975, aged 13 months. In 1994 she began her training at the Academy of Laboratory Technicians where she obtained a degree in chemistry. She then went on to gain her Masters degree in pharmaceutical chemistry completing the course in two years instead of three. She is now working in the laboratory of a pharmaceutical factory in Solo as an industrial pharmacist and lives in a boarding house nearby. She returns home to Beth Shan at week-ends continuing to produce beautiful cards and craftwork.

SABDINATOR

Sabdinator (Sab) was three-and-a-half years old when he joined the Beth Shan family in February 1976. He originates from the Dyak tribe in Kalimantan (Borneo). Due to his unwillingness to work and his influence on the other children the Yayasan decided in 1993 that he should return to Kalimantan under the care of the pastor who had asked Beth Shan to look after him.

After a long period away from the Lord he recommitted his life to God in 1996 and in August of that year started a two-year course at Bible College. Anne attended his graduation in July 1999. He is now working as an Assemblies of God pastor amongst his own people and has a powerful ministry.

YANTO

Yanto (Julianto) was brought to Beth Shan with his sister Lidia in 1976 when he was four years old and Lidia was three. They are both totally deaf although there is no history of deafness in the family. Yanto is very clever and is brilliant at painting. He has a great sense of humour and has accepted his disability. He works hard at everything he attempts and in 1995 completed a course in tailoring. He moved to Jakarta where he took a one-year advanced course in dress designing and passed with honours. All his grades are A's . He now has his own dress designing business and works from one room in the centre of Jakarta. His desire is to be totally self-supporting. The way forward will not be easy for him as in Indonesia people with disabilities are looked upon as second-rate citizens. In his early twenties he became a Christian and is keen to go on with the Lord in spite of the setbacks of communication. His sister, Lidia, is also in Jakarta where she is working as a hairdresser.

SRI SUWARNI

Sri Suwarni is the older sister of Lidia and came to Beth Shan in 1995 when she was seventeen years old. She had been desperately ill with typhoid fever and recovery was slow. She helped out at Beth Shan until entering Bible College in 1996 where she trained in village evangelism. She graduated in 1998 and spent a year in Sumatra in village outreach work. She is now working full-time as a staff member at Beth Shan and has tremendous insight into the lives of the teenagers.

RULI

Ruli was nine years old when he came to Beth Shan in 1984. He did well at school and went on to become a graduate of the Academy of Accountancy and Business Studies. Whilst waiting to find work he helped out at Beth Shan but now works until 2 p.m. each day in the administration department of a university in Solo. After a short break when he returns home he works at Beth Shan in the evening and lives in the staff quarters. He is hard-working and loved and respected by both children and staff. He is a keen musician, playing bass guitar in the services at Cemani Church and encourages the children to develop their musical talents. He was baptized in 1991.

LI SEN

Li Sen joined the Beth Shan family with his brother Cap Sen in January 1976 when he was two years old. He worked hard at school and obtained good results in his final exams. In 1993 he was accepted by Garuda Indonesian Airways for their Pilot Training School having done exceptionally well in his entrance exams. He was one of eleven finalists. He then started a three-year engineering course and was given a grant because of his excellent results and consistent commitment to study. He passed with high marks and Anne attended his graduation in Jakarta.

When Garuda Airways developed financial problems in 1997 Li Sen was amongst those made redundant.

On August 28th, 1999, he became engaged to Ester, now a trained nurse, who had joined the family in 1979 and on January 17th, 2000, they were married in Cemani church where the

Beth Shan family regularly worship.

They have recently moved to Jakarta looking for work. Both are totally committed to the Lord. Cap Sen is married with three children and is currently working as a sales rep.

LI MIN
Li Min is married with two children. She lives in Jakarta where her husband is a church planter. She works as a hairdresser.

EXPLANATORY NOTES

The Yayasan (Foundation Trust) is a legal body established by Dr. Pontas Pardede in 1972 to enable Anne to function as a missionary and to oversee the work that would develop. It has six members with Dr. Pardede as Chairman. Until Anne became an Indonesian citizen in 1989 she had no legal rights. The role of the Yayasan is currently under review due to changes in the political situation and in legislation.

Cemani Village where the Beth Shan Orphanage is located is on the outskirts of the city of Solo (Surakarta).

Cards and Crafts began as a Christmas card competition in 1989. The children are encouraged to use their craft skills to produce beautiful cards and crafts which are then sold. This 'self-help' scheme continues to develop with sales outlets in many places in Central Java and in the U.K. Each child has an individual bank account which is credited with all they have earned to go towards their college/university costs with Anne continuing to pay half the amount involved. The children are also rewarded for their efforts, receiving a bonus of £1 for every £10 of goods sold which they can spend as they wish. If a child is academically incapable of higher education the money they raise can be used for alternative education.

Finance. Although a registered orphanage Beth Shan receives no State aid. Medical and educational costs are high. Anne does receive help from a Christian doctor who gives her services without charge. A very generous monetary gift enabled the building of Beth Shan in Cemani village to commence and gifts of materials as well as money began to arrive. Rice has been given in large and small quantities over the years and always God has provided sufficient for the day. The number of people giving regular financial support continues to grow. Often Anne has been overwhelmed by the generosity of individual people as well as gifts from churches and organisations.

The following financial summary for 1981 makes interesting reading. A total sum of approximately £19,489 was received in gifts. Here is a brief account of how it was spent:

	£
Tithe	1,948.91
Wages	2,023.00
Medical expenses	1,612.70
Office expenses	937.25
Food	1,502.40
Milk	608.00
Maintenance	888.75
School fees and books	584.10
Building materials for Poniman's and Mesdi's houses and fish pond	5,438.00
Builders' wages	2,213.00
Miscellaneous	283.54
Robbed	250.00
Backdated bills	467.80
Electricity	257.90
Pedicab fares	<u>180.00</u>
Total	19,195.35

LINK CHILD

Link Child was set up by Audrey Corser (now Audrey Mann) during her stay at Beth Shan. Her vision was to find a prayer partner for each child without involving any financial commitment.

With new children always arriving there is a great need for people who feel able to do so to help in this very practical way. The main desire is for each child to be covered in and protected by prayer. News about a particular child can be provided on request.

A letter, birthday card, or small gift can give tremendous pleasure and comfort to a rejected or lonely child and tells them that someone cares!

Many have faithfully prayed for Anne and the work at Beth Shan from the beginning and regularly receive her prayer-letter. The effect of those prayers cannot be measured.

New prayer supporters are always an encouragement and if you are interested Anne would be delighted to hear from you.

Sheila Few has now taken over from Audrey the responsibility for Link Child.

Her address is:

Mrs. Sheila Few,
2 Charlotte Close,
Andover,
Hants
SP10 2PQ

'OPERATION DORCAS'

Operation Dorcas has come into being as a result of a substantial gift from a church in Fordham given specifically for the poor and not for Beth Shan. It is a family outreach scheme for local people and provides food and medication for those genuinely in need as well as sponsoring children through school with voluntary donations from the children of Beth Shan. Anne, and her colleague Mavis Pardede, have opened a bank account and named it 'Aksi Dorcas' (Operation Dorcas). This fund is used to help both Muslims and Christians who are in dire straits to start a small business – perhaps to buy a sewing machine, or learn to drive so that they can become independent and support their families. With reference to those who qualify for help thorough investigations are adhered to.

SPECIAL DATES FROM THE BETH SHAN DIARY

June 28th 1975 Anne moved into Beth Shan at Baron

May 10th 1978 Family moved into the 'new' Beth Shan

October 12th 1979 Tutik's wedding day

June 2nd 1980 Kindergarten School dedicated

October 1981 Work began on building the village church

June 1985 Work started on a second storey at Beth Shan

September 3rd 1986 Foundations laid for house at Kopeng

December 1987 First phase of Kopeng project completed

February 1988 Kopeng project completed

January 1989 Anne took the Oath of Allegiance

January 1995 Second storey at Beth Shan completed

August 28th 1999 Twenty-fifth Anniversary celebrations.

INDEX